MW00989709

ChinaCONDENSED

ChinaCONDENSED

5000 years of history and culture

Ong Siew Chey

Marshall Cavendish
Editions

Series Editor: Melvin Neo
Designer: Lynn Chin Nyuk Ling

Published by Marshall Cavendish Editions
An imprint of Marshall Cavendish International
I New Industrial Road, Singapore 536196

Other Marshall Cavendish Offices:
Marshall Cavendish Ltd. 5th Floor, 32-38 Saffron Hill, London EC1N 8 FH, UK • Marshall Cavendish
Corporation. 99 White Plains Road, Tarrytown NY 10591-9001, USA • Marshall Cavendish
International (Thailand) Co Ltd. 253 Asoke, 12th Flr, Sukhumvit 21 Road, Klongtoey Nua, Wattana,
Bangkok 10110, Thailand • Marshall Cavendish (Malaysia) Sdn Bhd, Times Subang, Lot 46, Subang
Hi-Tech Industrial Park, Batu Tiga, 40000 Shah Alam, Selangor Darul Ehsan, Malaysia

Marshall Cavendish is a trademark of Times Publishing Limited

National Library Board Singapore Cataloguing in Publication Data

Ong, Siew Chey.
China condensed : 5000 years of history and culture / Ong Siew Chey. – Singapore : Marshall
Cavendish Editions, c2008.
p. cm.
Includes bibliographical references and index.
ISBN-13 : 978-981-261-619-7 (pbk.)
ISBN-10 : 981-261-619-5 (pbk.)

1. China – Civilization. 2. China – History. I. Title.

DS706
951 -- dc22   OCN232616670

Printed in Singapore by KWF Printing Pte Ltd.

P R E F A C E

This book is not an in-depth study of Chinese history and culture. Various aspects of the Chinese identity have been dealt with in numerous books written by both Chinese and Western authors. Many present detailed information with perceptive interpretations, leaving serious students of Chinese history and culture with no lack of sources of information and reference.

This book was written for a different audience: young overseas Chinese, as well as non-Chinese, who would like to have at least a nodding acquaintance with Chinese history and culture. They might find the task of ploughing through one of the thick, well-researched books rather daunting. Furthermore, the uninitiated may find it difficult to unravel China's complicated past or to gain basic knowledge of a seemingly mysterious culture. This book is an attempt to present basic information about the Chinese in a simple way; it is by no means thorough or comprehensive.

The interpretations of aspects of Chinese history and culture presented here do not necessarily conform to conventional opinions. Recent history following the founding of the People's Republic of China is not covered in great detail here, as the facts are well known and readily available.

CONTENTS

CONTENTS

CONTENTS

CHRONOLOGY

?? B.C. – 1122 B.C. ◼ **The Legends Period**
⬝ The Xia (夏) Dynasty (2205 B.C. – 1766 B.C.)
⬝ The Shang (商) Dynasty (1766 B.C. – 1122 B.C.)

1122 B.C. – 221 B.C. ◼ **The Zhou (周) Dynasty**
⬝ The Western Zhou Dynasty (1122 B.C. – 770 B.C.)
⬝ The Eastern Zhou Dynasty (770 B.C. – 221 B.C.)
⬝ The Spring-Autumn Period (770 B.C. – 476 B.C.)
⬝ The Warring States Period (476 B.C. – 221 B.C.)

221 B.C. – 206 B.C. ◼ **The Qin (秦) Dynasty**

206 B.C. – 220 ◼ **The Han (汉) Dynasty**
⬝ The Western Han (206 B.C. – 9)
⬝ The Eastern Han (25 – 220)
⬝ The Three Kingdoms Period (220 – 264)

256 – 420 ◼ **The Jin (晋) Dynasty**

420 – 589 ◼ **The South-North (南北朝) Dynasty**

589 – 618 ◼ **The Sui (隋) Dynasty**

618 – 907 ◼ **The Tang (唐) Dynasty**

960 – 1279 ◼ **The Song (宋) Dynasty**
⬝ The Northern Song Dynasty (960 – 1127)
⬝ The Southern Song Dynasty (1127 – 1279)

1279 – 1368 ◼ **The Yuan (元) Dynasty**

1368 – 1644 ◼ **The Ming (明) Dynasty**

1644 – 1912 ◼ **The Qing (清) Dynasty**

1912 – 1949 ◼ **The Republic of China**

1949 ◼ **The People's Republic of China**

MAP OF CHINA

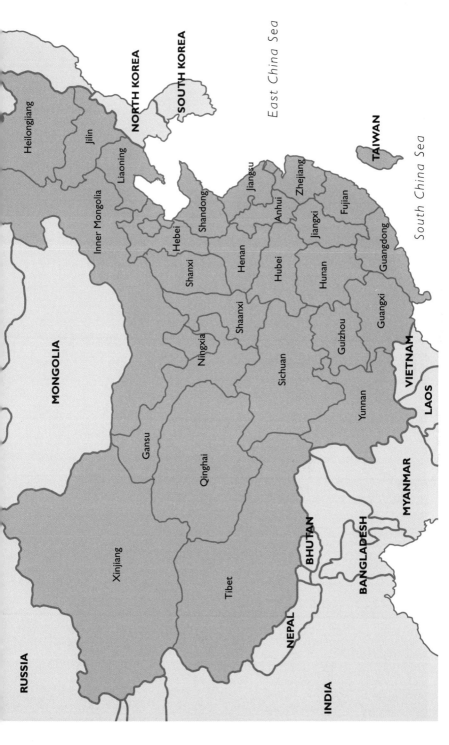

HISTORY

FROM LEGENDS TO RECORDS

Ancient Mythology

Chinese mythology surrounding the creation of the universe includes a legend that begins with a god named Pangu (盘古) awakening from a long sleep to find himself within a dark, undifferentiated, egg-shaped mass. Taking an axe, Pangu splits the mass. The lighter, clearer elements that had once been part of the mass float upward to become heaven. The heavier, coarser substances settle down to become Earth. A goddess named Nüwa (女娲) then appears. Disliking the barrenness of the earth, she proceeds to make the first human beings from clay. That is the beginning of the earth and human history.

The Yellow Emperor: Primal Ancestor of the Chinese

The Chinese consider the Yellow (黄) Emperor a primal ancestor and call themselves the descendants of the Yellow Emperor. The Yellow Emperor's reign presumably began in 2704 B.C. He conquered the tribes along the Yellow River to form the first kingdom of China. However, the Chinese sometimes also consider the Yan (炎) Emperor, a powerful tribal leader subdued by the Yellow Emperor in a battle, as another primal ancestor.

Legend has it that the Yellow Emperor reigned for 100 years. A succession of three or four little-known rulers ascended the throne after him over a period of some 200 years. Up to this point, Chinese history consists mainly of legends.

The first king who can be identified with some degree of certainty following the period is Yao (尧).

THE LEGENDARY RULER

The Yellow Emperor left no archaeological artefacts to speak of, but legends about him abound. He is supposed to have introduced the use of herbal medicine to treat ailments and invented the carriage and the compass, among other things. The Yellow Mountain in the province of Anhui (安徽) owes its name to this emperor, for he had supposedly concocted herbal remedies there.

The Xia (夏) Dynasty (2205 B.C. – 1766 B.C.)

In 2357 B.C., about 250 years after the Yellow Emperor's reign, a man named Yao became the ruler of China. Known as a benevolent king, he governed the people with kindness and wisdom. He passed the throne to Shun (舜), the best man he could find, instead of his own son. As a king, Shun proved to be as kind and wise as his predecessor. He too chose not to make his son his successor, instead choosing a man named Yu (禹) to become the next king in 2205 B.C.

Before he was chosen to become king, Yu had spent 13 years battling widespread floods in the country, eventually taming the rivers through diversion and drainage. Such was his dedication to duty that he left his home to perform this task on the fourth day of his marriage, never once returning until he succeeded in controlling the floods.

When Yu died, his son took over the throne and founded the first ruling dynasty in China, the Xia (夏) dynasty. From this time on, the throne would pass to a son or a relation after a ruler's death, forming the basis for a dynastic system that would last some 4,000 years until the founding of the Republic of China in 1912. In the time following their reigns, Kings Yao, Shun and Yu were revered as sages and model rulers by all Confucian scholars.

The Xia dynasty was the beginning of the Bronze Age in China, which lasted more than a thousand years until the dawning of the Iron Age at the time of the Zhou (周) dynasty. Many of the sophisticated bronze wares and weapons unearthed during archaeological excavations in the province of Henan (河南) date back to the Xia period.

The Shang (商) Dynasty (1766 B.C. – 1122 B.C.) and
Early Written Language

The Xia dynasty ruled China for more than 400 years until the last king in the line, a tyrant named Jie (桀), was deposed by a tribal chief called Tang (汤). Tang went on to establish the Shang (商) dynasty, which lasted more than 600 years. The last Shang king, Zhou (纣), was an extremely cruel man. One infamous method of torture he was fond of involved slowly burning someone to death over a bronze pillar heated by fire. He committed suicide when rebels led by Ji Fa (姬发), the founder of the Zhou dynasty, cornered him.

The Chinese generally claim that their civilisation has a history that dates back 5,000 years. Recent archaeological finds have pointed to the possibility that it is much older. However, the earliest available written record of Chinese civilisation dates back only as far as the Shang dynasty.

The written language of the Shang period was accidentally discovered when engraved characters were noted on cattle bones unearthed by farmers. The bones were used for medicinal purposes before they were recognised for their archaeological significance. The excavation of Yin (殷) ruins in Henan province in the 1920s yielded an abundance of tortoise shells inscribed with the script of the Shang dynasty. There are more than 4,000 characters in this ancient language, of which some 2,000 have been deciphered. Chinese script has probably been in existence for thousands of years, since before the Shang dynasty, but the script had most likely been inscribed on bamboo and neither script nor bamboo appear to have survived the ravages of time.

Finds such as the bones and tortoise shells provide a reliable indication of the level of civilisation that existed during the Shang dynasty. The relics include oracle bones used by rulers to seek divine guidance. Some historical events as well as information regarding life in that era were also recorded on the tortoise shells. There is evidence of a calendar in use, and the people appear to have had some knowledge of astronomy and mathematics. The highly refined bronze wares, ceramics and jade ornaments unearthed at the ruins provide evidence that a fairly advanced civilisation existed in China during the Shang period. There is indication that commerce was well developed. This is perhaps the reason why the name for merchant in Chinese is "*Shang ren*" (商人) or "Shang man".

EARLY DOCUMENTED HISTORY

The Zhou (周) Dynasty (1122 B.C. – 221 B.C.)

As a practice that had been established as far back in time as the Zhou (周) dynasty, rulers would appoint official historians to record the events that transpired during their reigns. The most famous of these court historians was one Sima Qian (司马迁) of the Han (汉) dynasty. Sima had followed his father's footsteps in becoming a historian, and several of his ancestors had been court historians during the Zhou dynasty.

The history Sima compiled, known as *Shi Ji* (史记), or *The Annals*, stretches back to the time of the Yellow Emperor. While it is not clear what sources Sima based his work on, his account of the Shang period, more than a thousand years before his time, was proven accurate when the Shang oracle bones were unearthed and studied. It is possible that Sima had access to pre-Zhou dynasty historical records, which are now lost. The history of the Zhou dynasty, which followed the Shang, is considered well documented, as the Chinese language had by then developed to a high degree. Accurate and detailed records of events were kept and passed down, forming the basis for some of the great classics.

DICTATING THE PATTERN OF A CULTURE

Tradition holds that the pattern of traditional Chinese culture was set in the early Zhou dynasty when Zhou Gong (周公), regent for a young king, introduced *The Rites of Zhou* (周礼). These rules defined the proper etiquette for the different levels of officials in the kingdom, the different classes of people in society and the different generations in a family. Ceremonial music and dances for different occasions and for different social classes were specified. Zhou Gong's doctrine of hierarchy and status distinction subsequently influenced Confucius profoundly and formed a great part of Confucius' teaching, which in turn dominated traditional Chinese thought.

The Zhou dynasty reigned, although sometimes only in name, for the longest time in China, more than 800 years. For a long period, the central government under the Zhou king was weak, and a number of feudal lords practically ruled their territories as independent kingdoms.

In the early part of the Zhou dynasty, a king introduced the *fengjian* (封建) or feudal system of government. Seventy-one lords, most of whom were the king's relatives, were appointed and given territories to govern. They were obligated to pay tributes to the king and to come to his aid in the event of an invasion. In return, the king would protect an individual lord if he were attacked by his peers or other invaders.

As an inevitable consequence of the system, these lords gradually built up their military strength. Thus, for a great part of the Zhou dynasty, the feudal lords overshadowed the king and fought among themselves.

The Western Zhou Dynasty (1122 B.C. – 770 B.C.)

For the first 352 years of the Zhou dynasty, a period referred to as the Western Zhou dynasty, the capital was located near present-day Xi'an (西安). Because it was frequently attacked by nomads from the west, a chain of bonfire pads stretching from the capital into the countryside was built. When the bonfires, each one located a certain distance from the next, were set ablaze in succession, a summons for help could be quickly transmitted to feudal lords in the outlying areas. Ironically, this ingenious alarm system would contribute to the downfall of the Western Zhou dynasty.

The last king of Western Zhou was fascinated by a beautiful concubine who would not smile. None of his attempts to please her, to coax the slightest merriment out of her, met with any success. Having tried just about everything else, the king had the bonfires lit. Fearing the worst, the feudal lords and their armies rushed to the capital—only to discover that there had been no real threat. Obviously, they did not take well to this false alarm. However, the concubine, who had watched the scene unfold from her vantage point high atop a tower on the city walls, was greatly amused and finally laughed.

Some time later, nomads attacked the capital. The bonfires were again lit, this time to signal an actual invasion. Unfortunately, the feudal lords, wary of being tricked again, ignored the signal. Thus, no help came as the nomads proceeded to sack the capital and kill the king.

The Eastern Zhou Dynasty (770 B.C. – 221 B.C.)

After the death of the last king of Western Zhou, a new king moved the capital to Luoyang (洛阳), establishing the Eastern Zhou dynasty. Spanning more than 500 years through the reigns of 25 kings, this latter part of the Zhou dynasty was characterised by a weak central government. As the kingdom's various feudal lords gained in power, often overshadowing the king himself, conflicts among vassal states became more commonplace. Despite the turmoil, this period was an extremely dynamic time for Chinese culture.

Such great Chinese philosophers as Confucius (孔夫子) (551 B.C.) and Lao Zi (老子) (575 B.C.) lived during the Eastern Zhou dynasty. It was also at this time that Sun Zi wrote his famous treatise on military strategies, *The Art of War*, a book still studied in modern military academies across many countries. Interestingly enough, it was also the period when Sakyamuni (563 B.C.), the Indian founder of Buddhism, and Greek philosophers Socrates (469 B.C.), Plato (429 B.C.) and Aristotle (384 B.C.) were born.

Historically, the Eastern Zhou dynasty is divided into two periods: the Spring-Autumn period and the Warring States period.

The Spring-Autumn Period (770 B.C. – 476 B.C.)

The Spring-Autumn period derives its name from the historical record that chronicles some 244 years, from 770 B.C. to 476 B.C., of the Eastern Zhou dynasty, *The Spring-Autumn Annals* (春秋). Incidentally, the Chinese characters for "spring" and "autumn" combine to mean "age" or "passage of time", and indirectly "history" or "annals".

XI SHI (西施): THE ANCIENT MATA HARI

A celebrated tale of the Spring-Autumn period is that of Xi Shi, said to be the most beautiful girl in Chinese history.

The story begins with the state of Yue (越) losing a war to the state of Wu (吴). The Yue king was captured and made to work as the Wu king's servant. He swallowed his pride and served the Wu king in the lowliest way. When the Wu king fell ill, the Yue king tasted his excreta and cheerfully predicted a speedy recovery.

As time passed, the Yue king gained the trust of the Wu king and was allowed to return to his homeland. He lived an ascetic life to train himself for revenge. He found a beautiful girl named Xi Shi and presented her to the Wu king.

Xi Shi was trained for a double mission: to charm the Wu king so that he neglected state affairs and to convince him of the absolute loyalty of the Yue king. Xi Shi carried out her role so well that when the Yue king invaded Wu, the weakened, unprepared state was easily conquered.

Xi Shi's fate following the fall of Wu is a mystery. Some romantic historians claim that she was reunited with the Yue king's minister, who had masterminded the whole plot against Wu, and the two went into hiding in the Tai Lake area where they lived happily ever after.

The Spring-Autumn Annals

As had been mentioned previously, there were many vassal states that grew to prominence during the Eastern Zhou dynasty. Among them was Lu (鲁), the state in which Confucius resided. *The Spring-Autumn Annals* are actually a record of the history of Lu. The other states each had their own annals as well, but these records have since been lost. Because the annals of Lu also contain some references to the other states, they are taken to represent the history of the entire country at that period in time. It is the oldest Chinese historical record available for study today.

The identity of the person who wrote or compiled *The Spring-Autumn Annals* is a matter of some debate. Most scholars and historians credit the book to Confucius, supported by a quotation from *Mencius*, but not all of them agree with this hypothesis.

The original version of the book is sketchy and poorly edited and is of historical interest only. It was superseded by three different versions that are known to have been in existence since the Han dynasty. Of the three, the Zuo version (左传) is considered the most important and informative. It is credited by some historians to Zuo Qiuming (左丘明), a young contemporary of Confucius who is believed to have edited or interpreted the original work. Others think that someone who lived in the Han dynasty, a few hundred years later, was the real author of the Zuo version.

There appears to be no way to settle these academic differences over who may or may not have been the author or compiler of *The Spring-Autumn Annals.*

The Warring States Period (476 B.C. – 221 B.C.)

As the Eastern Zhou dynasty entered the period of the Warring States, which lasted 225 years, the many feuding vassal states in the kingdom had been reduced through internecine wars to seven. The seven states were essentially independent and only nominally subject to the control of the king of the weak central Zhou government. Two states would battle each other one moment and form an alliance against another the next before double-crossing each other.

Brave warriors, cunning military strategists and clever statesmen were very much in demand in the various states, which constantly strove for supremacy. A commoner with talent could rise to a high position once recruited into a state's intellectual ranks.

Intellectualism also flourished with "a hundred contending schools of thought" as philosophers jostled to put forth their views. The arguments, contentions and stratagems of the intellectual staff from the various states were later drawn from many sources and compiled over a few hundred years to become a classic collection of 486 anecdotes known as *The Strategies of the Warring States* (战国策).

JING KE (荆轲): THE ASSASSIN

Towards the end of the Warring States period, the state of Qin (秦) grew in power and began to annex the other vassal states. The prince of the state of Yan (燕), fearing a Qin invasion, recruited a swordsman named Jing Ke to act as an emissary to the Qin court. Jing Ke was to present to the Qin king a map of the territory that Yan would cede to Qin in return for peace. His real mission, however, was to assassinate the king.

It would not be easy to get near the king unless one were well trusted. Knowing this, Jing Ke went to visit a fugitive from Qin staying in Yan. The man had a handsome reward on his head and would have paid any price to have the Qin king dead. Once the fugitive learned of Jing Ke's mission, he committed suicide so that the swordsman could present his head to the Qin king. Hopefully, Jing Ke could then get near enough to the ruler to kill him.

The day arrived when Jing Ke had to leave for Qin. The prince of Yan bade him farewell by the Yi River and all who knew of his real mission came in white traditional Chinese mourning dress to see him off. The swordsman sang his famous farewell song:

The wind howls over the cold Yi waters.
风萧萧兮易水寒
The warrior leaves, not to return ever....
壮士一去兮不复还

Jing Ke was well-received in Qin. The king was particularly pleased to see the fugitive's head and allowed Jing Ke to ascend the royal dais to show him a map of the territory that Yan was offering to cede to Qin.

Jing Ke slowly unrolled the map scroll, in which a sharp dagger had been hidden. Using this weapon, he grasped the king's robe and stabbed. However, he missed his mark and the king broke loose. In the ensuing confusion, the king finally managed to draw his long sword, which had been stuck, and kill Jing Ke.

Soon after, Qin conquered Yan. The Qin king would later become the first emperor of China.

Xiongnu

Korea

Qiang

Qin

THE QIN (秦) DYNASTY (221 B.C. – 206 B.C.)

Qin Shi Huang: The First Emperor

The warring states of the Zhou dynasty fought one another incessantly, until eventually the state of Qin (秦), with its capital near present-day Xi'an, emerged the strongest.

In 246 B.C., Ying Zheng (嬴政), a 13-year-old prince, became the king of Qin. At first, he was content to let his ministers run state affairs. As he grew older, his extraordinary capabilities surfaced and he was soon recognised as a brilliant, but cruel, leader. By 221 B.C., at the age of 39, Ying Zheng had conquered the other vassal states, which by this time had been reduced to just six as a result of warfare. Ying Zheng established the Qin dynasty and called himself Qin Shi Huang (秦始皇), meaning "First Emperor", for he was truly the first person to unify China and form the first empire.

The Qin dynasty was very short-lived, lasting only 15 years. Qin Shi Huang himself occupied the throne for 11 years. He was succeeded by his son, who was murdered three years later. Qin Shi Huang's brother was then installed as emperor but the dynasty came to an end only a year later.

In spite of his relatively short reign, Qin Shi Huang's influence on China was very far-reaching. Westerners probably know more about the terracotta soldiers unearthed in his tomb than they do about the emperor himself. The emperor's numerous contributions made China a "modern" country in that era. However, his cruel nature and harsh rule caused untold hardship to the people, who soon rebelled. Like many brilliant dictators in the history of the world, Qin Shi Huang was both good and bad at the same time.

During the Warring States period, each state had its own written language, currency and system of weights and measures. Qin Shi Huang had his prime minister, Li Si (李斯), introduce a standard script for the whole nation. China might otherwise have been like India with many different written languages. Currency and weights and measures were standardised throughout the country. Carriages were all designed with uniform axle lengths so that the vehicles could travel on roads of a standard width. An elaborate system of highways was built, radiating from the capital near Xi'an to other parts of the country. In peacetime, foodstuff was transported with ease, and in war, soldiers were dispatched with speed. Inland waterways were improved to facilitate navigation and irrigation.

Prior to the Qin dynasty, the aristocracy enjoyed the privilege of inheriting official positions. For instance, when a district governor died, his position would automatically pass to his son. Qin Shi Huang abolished this system and established in its place a centrally controlled administrative system. All officials were appointed by the emperor. Each official, from the village level upwards, was responsible and accountable to the next highest ranking official, and ultimately to the emperor, in matters of tax collection, food production and such. This system of bureaucratic government was copied with modifications by most subsequent dynasties.

The other side of the coin was that Qin rule was extremely harsh, and punishment for any wrongdoing was inhumanely cruel. Qin Shi Huang was quite paranoid. He had all the weapons in the country confiscated to prevent rebellions. Offended by criticisms from Confucian scholars, he had 400 of them rounded up and buried alive. In order to have total control of people's minds, he ordered the burning of all books written prior to his dynasty. Books on medicine, divination and agriculture were spared. Some ancient records and classics, hidden in the walls of houses by scholars, escaped destruction but many other books were lost forever. Qin Shi Huang probably kept copies of the destroyed books in the palace. However, the palace was burnt to the ground when rebels subsequently conquered the capital.

The first emperor of China was obsessed with acquiring immortality and fell prey to many charlatans who offered him elixirs of life, most of which probably contained toxic ingredients. A few years before Qin Shi Huang fell ill and died at the age of 49 while on an inspection trip in the south, a charlatan named Xu Fu (徐福) had approached the emperor, claiming that he could find herbs of immortality on an island in the eastern ocean. He asked the emperor for ships, supplies, 500 young men and 500 young girls. They set sail but never returned. Legend has it that they reached Japan and colonised it.

Qin Shi Huang was a ruler who loved mammoth projects. Some two million labourers were conscripted to build the Great Wall of China, highways, an enormous palace and his colossal tomb ahead of his death. He did not build the entire Great Wall; he had the various defensive walls already in existence joined to form a continuous fortification spanning some 6,000 kilometres for defence against the nomads in the north. The end of the Qin dynasty, however, would have roots not from external threats but from within the country.

The End of the Qin Dynasty

Unable to endure the harsh rule of Qin, many peasants rose up against the emperor. The rebellion began when some 900 peasants conscripted into the army were being sent to a distant fortress. They were unable to meet the deadline set for their arrival because of bad weather and faced certain death as punishment for the delay. With nothing to lose, Chen Sheng (陈胜) and Wu Guang (吴广) led the desperate peasants in an insurgency and took over a nearby town. Joined by many other dissatisfied peasants, the group quickly gathered in strength and swept across several provinces. They were finally defeated by the imperial army. However, several better-organised rebel groups had sprung up by then and the capital soon fell into rebel hands.

The Chu-Han War

The rebel army that conquered the Qin capital in 206 B.C. was headed by a man of peasant stock named Liu Bang (刘邦). Liu founded the Han dynasty, displacing the Qin, but he did not have an easy time in his quest to become the emperor for he had a formidable competitor named Xiang Yu (項羽). Xiang Yu was an aristocratic general from the state of Chu (楚) and a ferocious warrior who initially won most of his battles with Liu. In the end, however, with help from able generals and clever advisors, Liu was able to turn the tide and defeat his intemperate and impetuous opponent, a man who did not heed his staff's good advice.

THE WAR THAT INFLUENCED A GAME AND INSPIRED AN OPERA

The Chu-Han War fought between Xiang Yu and Liu Bang lasted four years. The story holds great fascination for the Chinese. In Chinese chess, the dividing zone between the two sides of the chessboard is called the "Chu-Han Boundary", named after the Chu-Han War. Fans of Chinese opera would probably count as one of their favourites the poignant scene before the final battle where the warrior Xiang Yu bids farewell to his concubine. The concubine kills herself before he departs so that he can concentrate on the fighting without worrying about her. Later, when Xiang Yu is defeated and surrounded, he spots an old friend among the enemy soldiers. He kills himself to let the friend take his head and claim a handsome reward from Liu Bang.

THE HAN (汉) DYNASTY (206 B.C. – 220)

The Western Han (206 B.C. – 9)

The Han dynasty began in 206 B.C. and lasted more than 400 years. The earlier part of the Han dynasty is known as Western Han, when the capital was located in Xi'an. The capital was shifted to Luoyang to the east in the year 25 and the dynasty was called Eastern Han after that time. The continuity of the Han dynasty was interrupted temporarily between the Western Han dynasty and the Eastern Han dynasty when a high official usurped the throne for 15 years (9 – 24).

The first Han emperor, Liu Bang, possessed a suspicious and treacherous nature, and held doubts about the loyalty of the generals who had helped

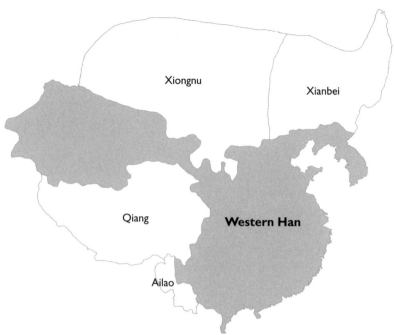

win him an empire. Some of them sensed the danger and rose up against him but were defeated and killed. In general, however, the first few Han emperors tried to ease the sufferings of the war-torn nation by lowering taxes and practising a mild rule. The country was generally well governed and gradually became prosperous.

Han Wu Di: The Emperor Who Expanded China's Territories

The most remarkable Western Han emperor, Han Wu Di (汉武帝), reigned from 140 B.C. to 86 B.C. He pursued both military and diplomatic strategies in his long-drawn war against the nomadic Xiongnu (匈奴) tribe. His outstanding generals repeatedly defeated the Xiongnu. At the same time, emissaries were sent deep into the western territory, known today as the province of Xinjiang (新疆), and beyond to form alliances against the Xiongnu. The first diplomat to be sent on such a mission, Zhang Qian (张骞), reached Afghanistan in 138 B.C. and came back with knowledge of the territories in Central Asia. This led to Chinese territorial expansion to the west and the creation of the famous Silk Road.

WANG ZHAOJUN AND THE XIONGNU

For many centuries, China proper was frequently invaded by fierce nomadic tribes, notably the Xiongnu, who roamed the northern and western fronts. Successive emperors tried to contain them to no avail. Even if they were sometimes defeated, the nomads would always return to do their plundering and killing. To appease them, some Han emperors even resorted to sending pretty palace maids and minor princesses to marry the tribal kings.

The most famous of these "lady diplomats" was Wang Zhaojun (王昭君), historically considered one of the four foremost ancient Chinese beauties. After marrying a northern tribal king in 33 B.C., she succeeded in having peace maintained in the frontier for a considerable time.

The story of Wang Zhaojun has remained a theme in Chinese operas, movies and songs till today. She is often depicted in paintings as a pretty girl dressed in fur on horseback heading for the vast Mongolian steppe with a retinue. She is usually shown carrying a musical string instrument called the *pipa* (琵琶), giving the impression that she introduced the *pipa* to the nomads. The truth is probably the opposite; the *pipa* was most likely an invention of the nomads or of the Middle East that was copied by the Hans.

The Silk Road

The Silk Road began in Xi'an, known as Chang'an (长安) in the old days. It was not a single road but a general name for all the passages between China and countries to the south and west. There were three important passages, the oldest of which was the Southern Route passing between the Kunlun Mountain Ranges and the Taklimakan Desert of Xinjiang to reach Pakistan, Afghanistan and Iran. The other two were the Northern Route (renamed the Central Route) passing south of the Tianshan Mountains, and the New Northern Route passing north of the Tianshan Mountains. These two routes led to the shores of the Caspian Sea and the Mediterranean Sea. The two greatest empires in the world in those days, China in Asia and Rome in Europe, came to know each other through the Silk Road.

The Silk Road was so named because silk, which originated in China, was exported in large quantities via this route to the West. In actual fact, the Silk Road also served other functions apart from trade; it facilitated cultural and technological exchanges between the East and the West and the spread of Buddhism and Islam into China.

The Eastern Han (25 – 220)

At the end of the Western Han dynasty, Wang Mang (王莽), a high official, usurped the throne for 15 years. He tried to implement a number of reforms but failed at the end. His policies led to widespread peasant uprisings. Eventually, Liu Xiu (刘秀), a royal descendant, reclaimed the Han throne and moved the capital to Luoyang. This second period of the Han dynasty is called Eastern Han.

Liu Xiu, whose imperial title was Han Guangwu Di (汉光武帝), was a capable emperor. He implemented an enlightened agricultural policy. His famed general, Ma Yuan (马援) quelled an uprising in the south and regained control of Vietnam, a territory that China ruled and later held as a protectorate until it was lost to France 18 centuries later. The Chinese writing system and the Chinese model of administration prevailed in Vietnam until the imposition of French colonial rule.

The subsequent emperors of the Eastern Han dynasty were either mediocre or incompetent, and the dynasty went into a steady decline. There was a brief revival of power when an emissary named Ban Chao (班超) was sent to regain control of Xinjiang in the year 76. He managed to form an alliance with a number of tribes and states and defeat the resurgent Xiongnu. The vast western territory was once again brought under Chinese rule. After that period, the dynasty declined.

The last few Han emperors were young children. In each reign, palace eunuchs and maternal relatives of the emperor would dominate the government. Their corruption and abuse of power landed the country in a shambles. With widespread peasant uprisings, regional warlords took the opportunity to carve up the country. The Eastern Han dynasty officially ended in the year 220.

The Three Kingdoms (220 – 264)

The peasants who rebelled against the Eastern Han dynasty were led by a Daoist named Zhang Jiao (张角). They wore yellow turbans in battle for identification and were known as the Yellow Turban Rebels (黄巾). Though extremely successful at the beginning, they were finally defeated by imperial troops and regional warlords.

The warlords then proceeded to fight one another to expand their individual domains, creating a situation very much like that of the Warring States. In the end, all but three of the warlords were eliminated. These remaining warlords formed three kingdoms with Wei (魏) in the north, Wu (吴) in the south-east and Shu (蜀) in the south-west.

In spite of its short duration, the Three Kingdoms period spawned more interesting tales than most other periods in Chinese history. The three states all had the ambition to conquer the entire country. Wei was endowed with natural resources and vastness of land. Wu enjoyed the geographical advantage of occupying the lower reaches of the Yangzi River. Shu was situated in the poorer mountainous regions and had mainly human resources to rely on, and it had to invade to survive. The three kingdoms employed very complicated deceptions and trickeries in their dealings with one another.

The most extraordinary character in this saga was Zhuge Liang (诸葛亮), the prime minister of Shu, an extremely clever military strategist with the ability to forecast weather. He tried to form an alliance against Wei with Wu but his own king, Liu Bei (刘备), ultimately upset his strategic plans. He later made six unsuccessful attempts to conquer Wei. Zhuge Liang has been greatly admired by generations of Chinese for his loyalty and ingenuity.

THE JIN (晋) DYNASTY (256 – 420) AND THE SOUTH-NORTH DYNASTY (420 – 589)

The Jin (晋) Dynasty

In the year 265, Sima Yan (司马炎), whose family had already been the *de facto* rulers of the Wei kingdom for many years, usurped the throne of Wei. He then conquered the other two states in the Three Kingdoms, Shu and Wu, to establish the Jin dynasty.

Once again, China was unified but the dynasty started off badly with an avaricious emperor. The second emperor was incompetent and the country was beset by widespread famine and a civil war waged among eight contentious princes. Five nomadic tribes, the most powerful of which was the Xiongnu, seized this opportunity to overrun the northern part of China. The capital of Xi'an was occupied and the reigning emperor captured. The Jin dynasty retreated to the south.

The following period was the most chaotic in Chinese history. In the northern part of the country, the nomadic tribes formed a total of 16 kingdoms. In the southern part, the reign of the Jin dynasty continued until the year 420, when it was followed by a succession of four kingdoms. Historians refer to this period of some 170 years as the South-North dynasty.

The South-North Dynasty (南北朝)

The Chinese nation is heterogeneous, comprising many ethnic groups. The Han majority traditionally occupied China proper, south of the Great Wall and east of

Xinjiang. The Xiongnu, who roamed the western provinces and an area known today as Mongolia, began to carry out raids into China proper from 200 B.C. These invaders had been soundly beaten during the reign of Han Wu Di but reappeared as a threat from time to time.

In the sunset years of the Jin dynasty, around the year 400, five nomadic tribes, the Xiongnu (匈奴) and the Jie (羯) from the north, the Xianbei (鲜卑) from the north-east, and the Di (氐) and the Qiang (羌) from the west, invaded the northern half of China proper. These invasions were different from the previous hit-and-run raids in that the nomadic tribes began to settle, in large numbers and on a permanent basis, on the lands they acquired.

The northern part of China proper consequently became a melting pot of the various ethnic groups. The nomads learned agriculture from the Hans, who in turn learned cattle-farming from the tribes. Intermarriage was common and cultural assimilation occurred as well. The culture of the Hans, being more advanced than that of the other ethnic groups, generally prevailed.

Thus, although some small nomadic groups had much earlier crossed the Great Wall to settle in some parts of northern China proper, the South-North dynasty marks the beginning of extensive cultural and ethnic assimilation between the various northern and western nomadic ethnic groups and the Hans.

Another remarkable phenomenon of the South-North dynasty was the flourishing of Buddhism throughout the country. Numerous temples and countless grottoes with statues of Buddhist deities were built. A king in the south even gave up his throne to become a monk.

The Xiongnu

The Xiongnu had roamed the northern and western parts of China as far back as the Qin dynasty. They remained mainly nomadic until the South-North dynasty when those in the north crossed the Great Wall and began to settle down and mingle with the Hans. They were assimilated and eventually lost their ethnic identity. The Xiongnu in the western part began a migration into Europe where they caused havoc in the fourth and fifth centuries. They were known as the Huns, with Attila being their most famous leader.

HUA MULAN: A GIRL IN WARRIOR'S GARB

One well-known tale originating in the period of the South-North dynasty is that of Hua Mulan (花木兰), a young girl from a northern tribe who disguised herself as a boy and fought in a war that lasted 12 years.

Mulan's ageing father had been drafted into the army and her brother was too young to take his place. So, Mulan joined the army in place of her father. *The Ballad of Mulan* by an unknown author contains the following verse:

... My father has no grown son;

    阿爷无大儿

Mulan has no elder brother.

    木兰无长兄

Buy me a horse with saddle and all,

    愿为市鞍马

And I will go to war for my father....

    从此替爷征

Mulan returned home after 12 years in the army. Her comrades with her were utterly astonished when she went into her room and re-emerged in female attire.

THE SUI (隋) DYNASTY (589 – 618)

The Beginning of the Civil Service Examination System

The 16 northern kingdoms of the South-North dynasty eventually came under the rule of Northern Wei. Yang Jian (杨坚), an aristocrat of mixed Han-Turkish ancestry, conquered both northern and southern China and once again unified the country. He established the Sui dynasty in the year 589 and took the imperial title Sui Wendi (隋文帝).

Sui Wendi's reign was characterised by good order and prudence in spending. He was an able administrator, introducing a legal code, a government bureaucracy and a system of land distribution. Sui Wendi's most important and far-reaching innovation, however, would have to be the introduction of the civil service examination system, also referred to as the imperial examination system.

Under this system, scholars hoping to join the civil service would compete in an examination at the local level to win a place at the provincial examination. The successful candidates at the provincial examination would then go to the capital to take part in the metropolitan examination. Scholars who excelled in the metropolitan examination would be awarded places in the civil service according to their merits.

Through the practice of meritocracy, the civil service examination system made it possible for commoners to gain high positions in the government, which were once restricted to aristocrats. In a way, the civil service examination system fostered fairness in society. It was adopted by all of the later imperial Chinese dynasties and maintained for 13 centuries until 1905, towards the end of the Qing (清) (Manchu) dynasty.

While the civil service examination system enabled the government to discover and make use of talent, it was also responsible to a large extent for keeping China backward in science. The restrictive and conservative examination syllabus bound the scholars mainly to literary studies.

Sui Yangdi: The Emperor with a Dubious Reputation

The first emperor of the Sui dynasty was succeeded by his second son, Yang Guang (杨广), whose imperial title was Sui Yangdi (隋炀帝). He reigned from 604 to 618. As a young prince, he commanded an army half-a-million-strong and conquered southern China for his father. As an emperor, he built the 1,800-kilometre-long Grand Canal. It joined Beijing (北京) in the north to Hangzhou (杭州) in the south and linked five eastward river systems. The Canal greatly improved north-south transportation, promoted trade and facilitated military control of the south.

During Sui Yangdi's reign, the capital was moved from Xi'an to Luoyang. The latter was more central in location and had easy access to the Grand Canal. It soon became the largest commercial city in the dynasty.

The downfall of Sui Yangdi began when he lapsed into irrational behaviour. He had a very luxurious palace built by a huge labour force and, when the palace was complete, filled it with a number of pretty concubines. The Canal was used for a pleasure cruise to Yangzhou (扬州) in the south with an entourage of more than 200,000. Obsessed with the company of pretty ladies, the emperor acquired the dubious distinction of being the greatest imperial womaniser in Chinese history.

Sui Yangdi was also keen on territorial expansion. He successfully regained control of the western provinces. He also launched three successive large-scale invasions of Korea but was met with disastrous defeats each time. Near the end of his reign, his exploits brought misery to the people. A rebellion broke out and he was killed, bringing an end to the Sui dynasty, which only lasted a total of 29 years.

THE TANG (唐) DYNASTY (618 – 907)

Tang Taizong: The Enlightened Emperor

In the year 618, Li Yuan (李渊), a northern provincial governor, overthrew the Sui dynasty and became the first emperor of the Tang (唐) dynasty. He conquered the country largely with the help of his second son, Li Shimin (李世民).

Infighting broke out among Li Yuan's three sons eight years later. The ambitious Li Shimin killed his two brothers and forced his father to abdicate. He became the emperor himself, taking the imperial title Tang Taizong (唐太宗). He proved to be an enlightened ruler and the country became remarkably prosperous and strong under his reign. From that period on, overseas Chinese have often been called "Tang people".

Tang Taizong, unlike the first emperor of Han, trusted and rewarded the people who had helped him secure his empire. He also understood the importance of cultivating popular support. His well-known exhortation to his sons was: "The emperor is like a boat, and the people are like water. Water can carry the boat and can also sink it". He valued talent, which he selected through the civil service examinations. He carried out extensive administrative reforms, promoted education and introduced well-defined laws. The penal code of Tang was a modification of that of Sui but it was more coherent and lenient. The laws were rather humane by old Chinese standards. For instance, a death sentence must be reviewed three times and delayed for three days before it could be carried out. An unfair part of the code was that it treated the various social classes differently.

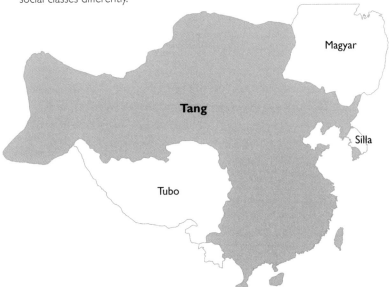

Tang Taizong's reign was marked by phenomenal prosperity. The capital Chang'an (Xi'an) had a population of more than a million and was undoubtedly the largest cosmopolitan city in the world at that time. In addition to traders, there were foreign students from Japan, Korea and other neighbouring countries at the city.

Two of the political and social reforms introduced by Tang Taizong were especially noteworthy. He modified the Sui government bureaucracy so that it resembled a cabinet system. On top were three senior ministries, one of which was charged with policy-making. A second ministry with censorial power would review and vet the policy before submitting it for imperial approval. It would then be passed to a third senior ministry with executive functions to be implemented through one of its six junior ministries. Another reform was to "nationalise" uncultivated and unclaimed land and to redistribute it to able-bodied farmers. Although aristocrats continued to enjoy a certain degree of privilege, the "equal field" policy was suggestive of an early socialist system.

A CHINESE PRINCESS FOR TIBET

In the year 629, during the reign of Tang Taizong, Srong-btsan Sgam-po (松赞千布) became the ruler of Tibet. An able monarch, he expanded the territory and introduced the first Tibetan script. He sought cultural exchanges with China and sent an emissary to the Tang court to request a matrimonial alliance. Tang Taizong obliged and had Princess Wen Cheng (文成) marry him. The princess brought with her an elaborate dowry as well as vegetable seeds, agricultural tools and books. She also brought along craftsmen to pass on Chinese technological advances. She was a Buddhist, and this prompted the Tibetan ruler to build a temple for her although Buddhism did not really take off in Tibet until the eighth century.

Wu Zetian: The One and Only Ruling Empress

In the year 637, Tang Taizong took a pretty 14-year-old girl into the palace. She was called Wu Zetian (武则天). She was spotted by the heir apparent to the throne. Upon the death of the emperor in 649, the prince ascended the throne. After she had spent a decent period as a Buddhist nun in a convent, Wu Zetian was asked by the new emperor, Tang Gaozong (唐高宗), to grow her hair back and re-enter the palace as a concubine. She bore him four sons and one daughter. All subsequent Tang emperors were actually her descendants.

Tang Gaozong ruled for 34 years but was troubled by poor vision in his old age. Wu Zetian practically ran the state affairs and became *de facto* ruler. After Tang Gaozong's death, the ambitious queen mother simply took over the throne from her young son in 690 and became the one and only empress to rule China in name and deed.

Wu Zetian was an excellent ruler. Externally, the western and the northern frontiers were regained. Internally, peace and order prevailed in the country, and the people were generally happy and satisfied. She was very keen to secure the best talents for the government, and she took a personal interest in running the traditional civil service examinations for scholars. Cheating by candidates and corruption of examiners were stamped out. In addition, she set up a new examination system for warriors in order to cultivate future generals.

Some semblance of democracy was introduced as the empress installed a suggestion box to receive suggestions, complaints and criticisms. Indeed, Empress Wu did a better job governing China than most emperors. It was probably in her reign that Chinese women became quite liberated. They rode horses and wore dresses with plunging necklines as shown by Tang pottery figurines. Critics of the empress, male chauvinists perhaps, often cited her sexual indulgence with disdain. Indeed, she was rather indiscreet when young and as reigning empress kept handsome young men in the palace for her pleasure.

Tang Xuanzong: The Love-Struck Emperor

Empress Wu stepped down in the year 705. Her son, the rightful heir, reclaimed the throne. In 713, the throne was passed to Tang Minghuang (唐明皇), also known as Tang Xuanzong (唐玄宗).

Basically an intelligent and capable monarch, Tang Xuanzong selected brilliant officials as ministers and eliminated redundancy in bureaucracy. He checked the rapid proliferation of Buddhist temples, which was draining the country financially.

However, his romantic nature got the better of him as he fell desperately in love with the famous royal concubine, Yang Guifei (杨贵妃). He bestowed favours on her entire family; her cousin was made prime minister and her three sisters became extremely wealthy and influential. He began to neglect his royal duties, passing the responsibilities of government to the corrupt prime minister, while he obsessively enjoyed the company of the stunningly beautiful lady. A Tang poem says:

> ...And thence, the emperor ceased to hold morning court,
> 春宵苦短日高起,
> For sunrise was untimely; the night was too short....
> 从此君王不早朝.

The concubine loved fresh lychees, which were grown in southern China. The fruit was carried more than 1,500 kilometres to arrive fresh at the capital Xi'an by what must have been the world's first pony express.

The country soon became a shambles. An Lushan (安禄山), governor and warlord of the northern provinces, rebelled and occupied the capital. The emperor was forced to flee to Sichuan (四川). Not far from the capital, the imperial army refused to march further until the emperor had all of Yang Guifei's relatives killed. Still, the soldiers were not pacified. The emperor finally had to have his beloved concubine strangled to death.

A few years later, An Lushan was killed, and the emperor returned to the capital. Broken-hearted, he abdicated and retired to reminisce about his favourite concubine. A long, sentimental poem written about their romance by the famous Tang poet Bai Jüyi (白居易), entitled The Song of Eternal Sorrow (长恨歌), is still widely read.

THE SEA SILK ROAD

Towards the end of the Tang dynasty, travelling along the Silk Road became a hazardous undertaking as nomadic tribes stepped up their attacks. Improvements in shipbuilding and the use of the compass paved the way for the rise of an alternative Silk Road—on the sea. This sea Silk Road extended from the south-eastern ports of China to the Middle East by way of South-East Asia. As the sea Silk Road assumed more importance, many Arab merchants even began to settle in those Chinese ports.

The Decline of the Tang Dynasty

The last part of the Tang dynasty was characterised by pleasure-seeking emperors who exploited the people in every way. In 875, Huang Chao (黃巢), a scholar who had failed the imperial examination, led a peasant uprising that was initially very successful. The rebels even managed to capture the capital before imperial troops defeated them in 884. By that time, the central government had become so weak that regional warlords had begun to assert themselves and undermine imperial power. The Tang dynasty ended in 907. A succession of five short dynasties followed, lasting a total of 54 years. In addition, the periphery of the country fragmented into ten small independent states, resulting in chaos. This era is known as the Five Dynasties and Ten Kingdoms period (907 – 960).

THE SONG (宋) DYNASTY (960 – 1279)

The Northern Song Dynasty (960 – 1127)

The Five Dynasties and Ten Kingdoms period eventually gave way to unification. Zhao Kuangyin (趙匡胤), a general who had served the last of the five short dynasties, took over the throne in 960 and conquered most of the ten kingdoms, establishing the Song dynasty, historically known as Northern Song. Zhao set up his capital at Kaifeng (开封).

However, a large part of northern China was occupied by the Liao (辽) tribe, arising from western Manchuria and eastern Mongolia. Zhao found it difficult to dislodge the tribe and the situation persisted into the reign of the second Song emperor, Zhao's brother. The Liao were now firmly entrenched in the north. Eventually, the emperor accepted the standoff and signed a peace treaty with the Liao, paying them a handsome yearly tribute.

While the Northern Song dynasty was preoccupied with the Liao, another tribal group that originated from the Qiang (羌) tribe intruded into the western territory and established a kingdom called Western Xia (西夏). The Song emperor was forced to recognise the kingdom and pay a yearly tribute to Western Xia to ensure a peaceful coexistence.

Economic and Cultural Advances during the Northern Song Dynasty

Despite being militarily weak and having to share the country with two other kingdoms, the Northern Song dynasty managed to achieve impressive progress in many fields.

Barter trade was largely eliminated in favour of a money economy using copper and silver coins, letters of credit and several types of paper money. Trade flourished as a result. New technology also emerged in coal and iron smelting, the design of agricultural tools, the weaving of textiles and the making of ceramics.

Such developments extended into the field of literature as well. While the Tang dynasty is famous for its poetry of standard formats, the Song *ci* (词) verse with its many variations is lively and refreshing. Today, Chinese school children are still taught some of the more popular Song verses.

THE WARRIOR WOMEN OF THE YANG FAMILY

The legendary Yang family (杨家将) of the Song dynasty produced three generations of warriors for the long-drawn Liao campaign, several of whom died in action. Legend has it that when the family ran short of male generals, the wives and widows took over command of the army and carried on fighting. Their saga gave rise to several traditional Chinese operas.

Wang Anshi: The Reformist

Even though a number of remarkable achievements were made in many fields during the Song dynasty, the country remained badly governed. A clear danger loomed on the horizon and the situation needed to be remedied.

Thus, Wang Anshi (王安石), the prime minister, implemented a series of reforms in 1069 with the emperor's blessing. Among some of the measures he instituted were the granting of loans to needy farmers at low interest, the taxing of farms according to a system equally applicable to commoners, aristocrats and officials, and the buffering of market prices as well as the elimination of unscrupulous middlemen through direct government sourcing and sale of certain commodities. Wang Anshi's reforms also extended to military, administrative, and educational matters and irrigation projects.

While Wang Anshi's reforms met with initial success, he finally had to yield to conservative opposition 16 years later. The decline of the dynasty soon became inevitable.

The Fall of the Northern Song Dynasty

The reign of emperor Song Huizong (宋徽宗), which began in 1101, marked the beginning of the rapid downfall of the Northern Song dynasty. Song Huizong was a gifted artist but a useless, pleasure-seeking ruler. He even had a tunnel dug from his palace to a brothel for secret visits to a famous courtesan. Soon, several rebel groups launched uprisings and the country enjoyed little peace.

Around 1115, the Nüzhen (女真) tribe came to power in the north-eastern part of China commonly known as Manchuria. The tribe founded the kingdom of Jin (金) and conquered the neighbouring kingdom of Liao in 1125. Invading south the following year, the Nüzhen occupied Kaifeng, the capital of the Northern Song. Emperor Song Huizong and his newly crowned son were both captured and taken north. The Northern Song dynasty thus came to an end.

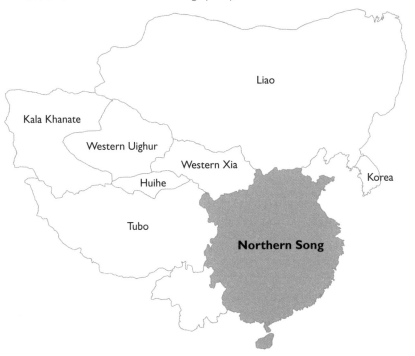

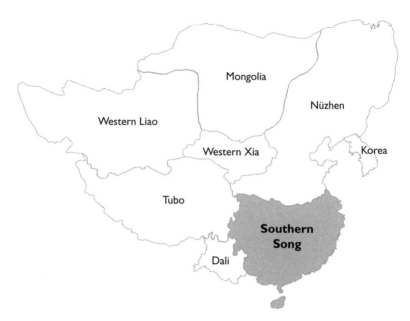

The Southern Song Dynasty (1127 – 1279)

With the end of the Northern Song dynasty in 1127, one of Song Huizong's sons escaped to the south and set up a continuation of the Song dynasty. The capital was established in present-day Hangzhou (杭州). This second period of the Song dynasty is referred to as the Southern Song dynasty.

The first Southern Song emperor was Song Gaozong (宋高宗). For many years the Nüzhen tribe invaded Southern Song frequently but it was held back by Song troops. Yue Fei (岳飞), an outstanding general, succeeded in driving the Nüzhen troops to an area near the Yellow River and was poised for the final attack.

However, the prime minister, Qin Gui (秦桧), wanted a peaceful settlement and persuaded the emperor to recall Yue Fei. Some say Qin Gui had probably been bribed by the Nüzhens to abort Yue Fei's campaign. Recently, historians have raised the possibility that Qin Gui could indeed have been acting under the emperor's instructions, as the emperor would not have been keen to see Yue Fei defeat the invaders; if Yue Fei were victorious, he would have brought back the emperor's father and brother, and the emperor would have had to give up the throne.

The emperor had to issue 12 recall orders before Yue Fei complied with imperial wishes, bearing in mind that it was an acceptable practice in old China for a general fighting in the field to ignore the emperor's orders. On Yue Fei's return to the capital, he was arrested, charged with treason and executed. His tomb at the West Lake of Hangzhou is frequented by visitors. Also at the tomb are statues of Qin Gui, his wife and two accomplices, all of whom had plotted against Yue Fei. It used to be customary for visitors to spit at the statues of the traitors.

Yue Fei is widely considered by the Chinese as a role model and a national hero because of his unflinching loyalty and his military prowess. While he was still only a boy, his widowed mother had tattooed onto his back four words, "jing zhong bao guo" (精忠报国), which can be translated as meaning "absolute patriotism". Throughout his life, Yue Fei remained true to his mother's teachings.

The Southern Song dynasty and the Nüzhen of the Jin kingdom fought to a standoff, maintaining a state of uneasy coexistence for many years until the rise of Genghis Khan and the Mongolians.

THE YUAN (元) DYNASTY (1279 – 1368)

The Mongolian Whirlwinds

In 1206, a Mongolian tribal leader who had consolidated all the Mongolian tribes, Temuchin, formed the Mongolian kingdom and became its Khan. He was called Genghis Khan, "The Invincible Khan". In subsequent years, his army conquered Jin-occupied northern China. At the same time, he started a wave of westward invasions that swept across northern India, Afghanistan, Persia, and from the Caucasus to the Black Sea. On his return to China in 1225, he invaded the Western Xia kingdom. He died in 1227 at the age of 66 on the eve of the surrender of Western Xia.

THE MONGOLIAN WRITTEN WORD

The Mongolians had no written language. It was during the reign of Genghis Khan when the Mongolian script was created.

Genghis Khan was succeeded by his third son, Ogödei, in 1229. Ogödei conquered the Jin kingdom and began a second wave of westward invasions. His army sacked Moscow before sweeping down Eastern Europe. The European nations hurriedly assembled a coalition army to meet the Mongolians. The battle would certainly have resulted in disaster for Europe, but before it could be fought, the Mongolian army mysteriously withdrew and returned home. Ogödei had unexpectedly died at home. Europe was spared further bloodshed.

Ten years later, in 1251, Möngke became Khan. His army invaded Southern Song, conquering most of the south-western part of China, but it became bogged down in the mountainous province of Sichuan. At the same time, another army embarked on the third wave of westward invasions and swept across the Middle East. It was on the verge of crossing the strip of land known as the Suez to attack Egypt and Africa when news was received that Möngke had been killed in the Sichuan campaign. Africa was saved.

In 1260, Kublai, grandson of Genghis, became Khan. He conquered Southern Song in 1279 and founded the Yuan dynasty, locating his capital at Dadu (Beijing). China was once again unified. By then, its territories had expanded to include Manchuria, part of Siberia, Korea, Eastern Europe and the Middle East. Administratively and militarily, the country was divided into four regions, or khanates, and each was ruled by a Khan, a descendant of Genghis.

THE "DIVINE WIND" THAT SPARED A NATION

In 1274 and again in 1281, Kublai Khan sent an invading fleet to Japan. On both occasions, the fleet was destroyed by typhoons. Japan was not conquered, thanks to the "divine wind" known as kamikaze.

Stubborn Resistance against the Mongolians

Kublai Khan did not conquer the remaining parts of China easily. There were some stubborn Song generals who refused to surrender. For instance, the Fishing City (钓鱼城) in Sichuan held off the Mongolians for 36 years.

The most well-known loyal Song official was Prime Minister Wen Tianxiang (文天祥) who, though a scholar, fought the Mongolians valiantly. He was much admired by Kublai Khan, who tried in vain to persuade him to surrender. He was finally captured and executed after four years of imprisonment.

The verse Wen Tianxiang wrote in prison, entitled *Upright Morality* (正气歌), is still studied in schools. The writing reflects typical Confucian teachings based on the theme of not compromising one's principles, even in the face of death.

The Mongolian Government

The Mongolians were nomads living in the vast steppes of Mongolia. They were excellent horsemen. An important factor in their military success was their extreme cruelty in dealing with the defenders once a city was taken. The entire population would be massacred, and this practice struck fear in the defenders of a besieged city, often causing them to flee or surrender when a Mongolian army appeared.

When the nomads settled down in China, they had to learn the ways of civilian government. Kublai Khan often took the advice of learned Hans. The early rapacious Mongolian rule was modified in favour of Chinese patterns of government and taxation.

However, Kublai could not overcome his arrogance. He divided the population into four classes. At the top were the Mongolians. Next came the people of Tibet, Xinjiang, the Middle East and Europe. The third class comprised Manchurians, Koreans and northern Hans. The southern Hans belonged to the lowest class. There was blatant inequality in the law, in the criteria for passing the imperial examination and in the appointment of civil officials. Military service was a Mongolian monopoly. These discriminatory policies prevented ethnic assimilation and the formation of a cohesive nation. They also planted the seeds of revolution among the under-privileged Hans. The Yuan dynasty lasted only 97 years in spite of its military might.

External Trade during the Yuan Dynasty

A remarkable development of the Yuan dynasty was the surge in external trade with the Middle East and the eastern coast of Africa via the sea Silk Road, which was first established in the Tang dynasty. Quanzhou (泉州), a port on the south-eastern coast, was a favourite trading post of merchants from Persia and Arabia. A mosque still stands there and Arab descendants are easily identifiable within the population. During this period, Chinese technologies such as printing and gunpowder were passed to Western Asia and from there to Europe.

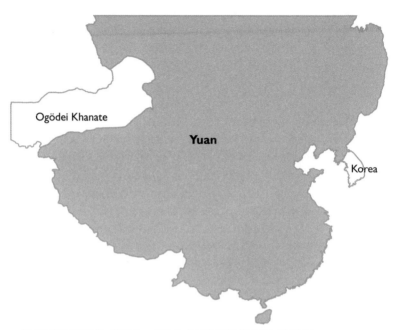

Ogödei Khanate

Yuan

Korea

MARCO POLO (1254 – 1324): A VENETIAN IN CHINA

Marco Polo was a Venetian. In the year 1271, at the age of 17, he undertook a journey by land to China with his father and uncle, and reached Beijing after three-and-a-half years. He stayed in China for 17 years, travelling extensively.

Kublai Khan took a liking to him and gave him a post in Yangzhou (杨州) where he stayed for three years.

He journeyed to Persia by sea from Quanzhou in 1292 and made his way back to Venice by land. However, he got caught in the middle of a war and was imprisoned for a year. During this time, he described his experiences in China to his cellmate, Rusticello da Pisa, a writer who presumably proceeded to write the original *The Travels of Marco Polo*. When the book was first published, Europeans were astonished to learn of the advanced civilisation that existed in China and many did not believe the stories within.

Rusticello's original script has long been lost although numerous editions of the book have appeared since then. There has been scepticism as to whether Marco Polo himself did go to China.

Perhaps there are inaccuracies and omissions in the book, which would not be surprising since it was based on Marco Polo's verbal account of his adventures. However, most Chinese believe that he did visit China. The description of his trip from Beijing to Yangzhou is too accurate to be hearsay.

The End of the Mongolian Empire
After Kublai Khan, the Mongolian Empire began to decline. Between 1308 and 1333, the dynasty went through a succession of eight emperors. By 1368, inept government and a series of natural disasters spelled a time ripe for a revolution, and the Ming dynasty displaced the Yuan.

THE MING (明) DYNASTY (1368 – 1644)

Zhu Yuanzhang: The Monk Who Became the Hongwu Emperor
Zhu Yuanzhang (朱元璋), the first emperor of the Ming (明) dynasty and most commonly referred to as the Hongwu emperor (洪武帝), came from an extremely poor family. When he was 17, his parents and siblings died in an epidemic, and he was left with no means of livelihood. He became a monk in a Buddhist temple just to survive. He was asked by senior monks to go out to beg for alms so as to lessen the burden of the temple. He travelled extensively in the country and the experience broadened his vision.

At the age of 25, Zhu Yuanzhang joined the rebel army fighting against the Yuan dynasty, later marrying the adopted daughter of the rebel chief. He rose to lead the rebellion and eventually toppled the Mongolian Empire. He founded the Ming dynasty in 1368 and became its first emperor. The capital was established in Nanjing (南京) at the southern bank of the Yangzi River.

Essentially a self-taught man, Zhu Yuanzhang learned to write well and could even compose poetry. His administration was honest and benefited the poor. Ming laws were clear and strict, and traditional Confucian values were restored. At the beginning of the dynasty, the country had been in disarray due to years of war. Farms were neglected, and the population had dwindled down to 60 million. Zhu Yuanzhang's government reversed the trend and the population more than doubled during the Ming dynasty.

The other side of Zhu Yuanzhang was not so flattering. He was distrustful, somewhat paranoid, and prone to irrational behaviour in spite of the moderating influence of his wife, Empress Ma. Several of the generals and advisors who had helped him build his empire were killed on suspicion of disloyalty. He divided the country into several regions, each governed by one of his sons. Apparently, he thought this would give him some measure of security on the throne as blood is said to be thicker than water.

Zhu Di: The Yongle Emperor and Founder of the Forbidden City

Zhu Yuanzhang had 26 sons. Zhu Di (朱棣), the fourth son, was considered outstanding. He fought alongside his father in the Yunnan (云南) campaign to clear the country of the last bastion of Mongolian resistance and was later given the important post of guarding the territory around Beijing against possible Mongolian resurgence.

However, despite his apparent merits, Zhu Yuanzhang did not choose to make Zhu Di his successor. The eldest son was made heir apparent, and when he died young, the grandson was chosen to be the next in line. Zhu Di was passed over, possibly because Zhu Yuanzhang suspected that he was a Mongolian. It was said that Zhu Di's mother, a Mongolian princess Zhu Yuanzhang took to be his concubine, could have already been pregnant before meeting the emperor.

When Zhu Yuanzhang died in 1399, his grandson, as the nominated heir, ascended the throne. The new ruler, generally referred to by his imperial title as the Jianwen emperor (建文帝), felt insecure with so many of his uncles commanding armies in the outlying areas. He proceeded to eliminate these potential opponents one by one by stripping them of military power.

Unfortunately for the emperor, these actions prompted Zhu Di to invade Nanjing and take over the Ming throne. As Zhu Di's troops entered the capital, the palace was ablaze but the Jianwen emperor was nowhere to be found. It was rumoured that he had disguised himself as a monk and escaped to wander around the country as a vagabond. Another story was that he had escaped to South-East Asia by boat.

Zhu Di, who is also known as the Yongle emperor (永乐帝), relocated the capital to Beijing in the north as his main concern was Mongolian resurgence.

He had one million soldiers stationed there. He also ordered 10,000 households to move to the new capital to boost its population. The walled city was expanded and a new palace complex, the Forbidden City, was built. Zhu Di also had the Grand Canal widened to facilitate transportation of grains from the rich farmlands in the south to feed the population in the north.

Zheng He: The Eunuch Who Became Admiral

In 1381, during the reign of Zhu Yuanzhang, a 10-year-old Muslim boy named Ma He (马和) was captured by the Ming army in Yunnan province. He was later castrated and placed as a eunuch in the household of Prince Zhu Di, who was then 25 years old. Ma He's name was changed to Zheng He (郑和).

In the years that followed, Zheng He's abilities were much appreciated as he fought alongside Zhu Di, first against the Mongolians in the north and later in the invasion of Nanjing. Through a long and close association, Zheng He became Emperor Zhu Di's confidant. He was said to be a huge man with an imposing appearance befitting of a military commander. He was also known as San Bao, possibly meaning "The Eunuch with Three Treasures" (三宝), as he was said to always carry in a small casket beneath his cloak the three desiccated parts of his castrated organs. More likely, San Bao (三保), written differently but sharing the same pronunciation as the other, was actually his childhood name.

Zhu Di began to build ocean-going ships in 1403. By 1405, the fleet was ready to set sail from Nanjing. Zheng He was appointed admiral in command of the armada with permission to issue imperial orders at sea.

The reason why Zhu Di built the ships and sent Zheng He on multiple voyages at great expense still remains a matter of conjecture. It may be that he wanted to track down his nephew, the deposed emperor, but that theory sounds far-fetched as there was no reason to look for the royal fugitive in such far-flung places as Calicut, India. Trade was another possible reason, but the amount of trade Zheng He engaged in did not justify the size of the navy or the distance the fleet sailed. Certainly, Zheng He had no intention to colonise any foreign land; he simply asked the kings he subjugated to pay tributes to the Ming court. Perhaps the elaborate voyages were intended to be a show of China's wealth and power.

China's Dominance of the Seas

The earliest recorded Chinese maritime activity dates back to the Qin dynasty, around 219 B.C., when Xu Fu went to look for herbs of immortality in the eastern ocean. In the Han dynasty, which followed the Qin, Chinese seafarers regularly sailed to South-East Asia and went as far as Indonesia. The invasions launched by Sui Yangdi against Korea were partly by sea with ships carrying a large army. By the Tang dynasty, Chinese foreign trade via the sea flourished and extended across the Indian Ocean to the African coast. It continued unabated through the Song dynasty in spite of frequent war. During the Yuan dynasty, Chinese merchants regularly sailed to the African coast. Sea travel to Persia was commonplace. So, when Zheng He led his fleet to the South Seas in 1405, he was not exactly in uncharted waters. The difference lies in the scale of the undertaking. An armada of 317 ships with 27,800 men on board took part in the first voyage.

The ships that Zheng He commanded were very advanced in design. The nine-masted core ships were called "treasure ships" and were enormous in size, measuring approximately 135 metres long and 57 metres wide. By contrast, the *Santa Maria* in which Christopher Columbus sailed 87 years later was only 26 metres long. Supporting the core ships were several types of smaller ships carrying horses, supplies, goods, craftsmen, doctors, interpreters and troops. The smaller five-masted warships and the eight-oared patrol boats were no less than 30 metres long.

From 1405 to 1432, Zheng He's fleet made seven voyages to the Indian Ocean. He used Malacca in present-day Malaysia and Calicut on the western coast of India as his main bases. The ships reached the Persian Gulf and the east coast of Africa, trading and subjugating a number of nations along the way. The rulers of these nations began to pay tributes to China. Several rulers and ambassadors went with Zheng He to visit China and pay their respects to the Ming emperor. The rebellious ruler of Sri Lanka was captured and taken to China but later released and sent home. The ruler of Sulu in the Philippines spent several years in China and died there.

Zhu Di died in 1425, but Zheng He was able to make a seventh voyage, his last, in 1432. He died the following year at the age of 62, either in Calicut or at sea. His tomb in Nanjing contains only his clothing.

After Zheng He's death, the reigning emperor banned all seafaring activities. The ships of the once-mighty armada were left to rot as China isolated herself. Most of the original records of Zheng He's voyages were destroyed but an account of the voyages is available today in a well-researched book by Louise Levathes, *When China Ruled the Seas.*

ZHENG HE FIRST, CHRISTOPHER COLUMBUS SECOND

Maritime historian Gavin Menzies, a former submarine commander in the British Royal Navy, has written a book entitled *1421: The Year China Discovered America,* which is based on the extensive research of ancient maps, shipwrecks, and museum and library records, complemented by the author's expert knowledge on oceans, currents, trade winds and astronomy. Menzies' startling thesis is that during Zheng He's sixth voyage, he divided the armada into four fleets. He went home with a small fleet. His deputies led the other three fleets all over the world for two-and-a-half years from 1421 to 1423, covering the Cape of Good Hope, the Straits of Magellan, Australia, Antarctica, both coasts of South America, Central America, both coasts of North America, Greenland and the Arctic Sea. Small groups of men were supposedly left behind in North and South America. All these activities purportedly took place long before Christopher Columbus discovered the New World. The evidence Menzies presents in support of his theory is difficult to refute although some of it may have been over-interpreted.

Matteo Ricci: The Jesuit Priest

The first European to introduce Western science to China was an Italian Jesuit priest named Matteo Ricci (利玛窦). He arrived in China in 1583 during the reign of the thirteenth emperor in the Ming dynastic line, Wanli (万历).

Sent to China primarily to convert the Chinese to Christianity, Ricci was extremely patient in trying to gain Chinese acceptance, friendship and recognition. He learned the Chinese language, wore Chinese attire and was thoroughly familiar with Chinese culture and customs. He aroused the interest and the curiosity of the Chinese with novelties such as clocks, prisms and sundials.

While preaching his religion, Ricci translated books on trigonometry and geometry into Chinese and gave the Chinese the first glimpse of Western mathematics. He also taught Western astronomy and geography, and published the first maps of China. He was later appointed court mathematician in Beijing.

He lived in China for 27 years and died there in 1610. One can still visit his tomb in a suburb of Beijing. In 1983, China celebrated the four-hundredth anniversary of his arrival in the country. A warm account of Ricci was published, and a commemorative stamp with his picture was issued.

The Decline of the Ming Dynasty

In the later part of the Ming dynasty, the emperors were decadent. They pursued their personal pleasures and left state affairs to rogue eunuchs and corrupt officials. The rapacious and exploitative regime was plagued by continual peasant uprisings.

Externally, the country was harassed by frequent Mongolian invasions from the north and by the plundering of Japanese pirates along the eastern coast. When General Qi Jiguang (戚继光) eliminated the coastal pirates in 1565, he was acclaimed as a hero. In 1586, Japan became unified and began to expand externally. Korea, then a Chinese protectorate, was invaded in 1591 and again in 1597. On each occasion, the combined Korean and Chinese army was able to expel the Japanese invaders.

However, these Ming achievements were like the last rays from a setting sun, harbinger of the darkness to come. Peasant rebellions soon became rampant. The two strongest rebel groups were led by Li Zicheng (李自成) and Zhang Xianzhong (张献忠). Using the slogan "equal land distribution, no taxation and no conscription", Li gained popular support as his troops swept across northern China. He occupied the capital at Beijing and put an end to the Ming dynasty in 1643. The last Ming emperor hung himself.

Wu Sangui: The General Who Led the Manchus into China

When the Ming Empire fell to the peasant rebels, one general was left in a fort at the eastern end of the Great Wall named Shanhaiguan (山海关). General Wu Sangui (吴三桂) commanded an army 40,000 strong at the fort, which

Woyela

Ilibali

Tatar

Korea

Ming

controlled the gateway into China proper. He refused to surrender to Li Zicheng and instead enlisted the help of the Manchus, eventually leading the Manchu army into China proper. The Manchus subsequently conquered the whole of China and founded the Qing (清) dynasty. It was said that Wu Sangui had decided to fight Li Zicheng when he learned that Li's men had taken his favourite mistress, Chen Yuanyuan (陈圆圆), in Beijing.

The Ming Loyalist Resistance Movement

Even after the Manchus had gained control of most of China, pockets of resistance formed by Ming loyalists persisted for a long time. The most famous among these loyalists was Zheng Chenggong (郑成功), also known as Koxinga. He occupied a large area around the Yangzi River and even laid siege to Nanjing. He was eventually defeated and in 1661 sailed with his army to Taiwan, which was then occupied by the Dutch. Zheng Chenggong drove away the Dutch and kept the Ming flag flying in Taiwan. He died in 1662, and 20 years after his death, the island fell to the Qing Empire.

THE RISE OF THE COLONIAL POWERS IN ASIA

In 1511, the Portuguese extended their influence to South-East Asia and occupied Malacca. They later plundered the south-eastern coast of China and occupied part of Macau in 1553. Several ports in Taiwan were also occupied. Then, Dutch colonists took Java in 1619 and defeated the Portuguese in Taiwan to take the island in 1642.

THE QING (清) DYNASTY (1644 – 1912)

The Resurgence of the Manchus

A tribe from north-eastern Manchuria, the Nüzhen, had established themselves as a power in twelfth century China when they formed the Jin kingdom and conquered the Northen Song. However, their territorial ambitions were extinguished in the thirteenth century when the Mongolians invaded and disbanded the tribe.

Towards the end of the Ming dynasty, Nurhachi, a Manchurian tribal chieftain, unified the various Manchurian tribes again, re-establishing the Jin kingdom in 1616. Nurhachi defeated a large Ming army and occupied several cities along the northern frontier of Ming. He later died in battle, but not before he modified the Mongolian script to create the Manchu written script. He was succeeded by his son, who changed the name of the kingdom to Qing and carried on harassing Ming's frontier.

When Wu Sangui led the Manchu army into China proper in 1643, a young Manchu king, Fulin (福临), and his regent decided to take this opportunity to begin a large-scale invasion. The Manchus eventually conquered China and established the Qing dynasty. The first reign under Fulin from 1644 to 1661 was called Shunzhi (顺治).

The Names of Chinese Emperors

The surname of the Qing emperors was Aixin Jueluo (爱新觉罗). They each had a personal given name. However, they were usually referred to by the names of their reigns.

The naming convention for Chinese emperors may be clarified here. Once inaugurated, an emperor would not use his personal name. In fact, it would be a crime to mention the emperor's personal name. He would have been known by the imperial title he chose, prefixed by his dynasty's name. Hence, the first emperor of China is usually referred to by his imperial title, Qin Shi Huang, and seldom by his personal name, Ying Zheng.

By the Han dynasty, it had become customary to have a name for the reign of each emperor. The practice was passed down to subsequent dynasties. For example, the second emperor of the Tang dynasty had the personal name Li Shimin, the imperial title Tang Taizong and the reign name Zhen Guan (贞观). In his case, the imperial title was used most. Historians may choose to refer to some emperors mostly by their personal names, such as Zhu Yuanzhang and Zhu Di of the Ming dynasty. However, the subsequent Ming emperors and all the Qing emperors, such as Kangxi (康熙), Yongzheng (雍正) and Qianlong (乾隆), are mainly referred to by the names of their reigns.

China under the Qing Dynasty

The reigns of the three Qing emperors, Kangxi, Yongzheng and Qianlong, were a period of unprecedented prosperity. China undoubtedly became the wealthiest nation in the world. The territory held by the country was only second to that during the Yuan dynasty under the reign of the Mongolians. However, the country went on a roller-coaster plunge towards the end of Qianlong's reign.

The Qing dynasty marked the second time China was ruled by non-Hans, the first being the Yuan dynasty. Many Hans were unhappy, especially when they were forced to shave the front part of their heads and grow pigtails. There was blatant ethnic discrimination in government policies. Han scholars indicated their displeasure directly or satirically in their writing, prompting the first few Qing emperors to launch harsh literary inquisitions. Many scholars were arrested and summarily decapitated. Thus, beneath the phenomenal prosperity of the regime, there was an undercurrent of discontent among the Hans.

Kangxi: The Remarkable Emperor

Kangxi ruled China for 61 years. He was remarkable not only for the length of his reign but also for his outstanding ability and magnanimity. The opposition from the Han people encountered in his reign was mainly fuelled by nationalistic feeling, for at that time the Hans did not consider the Manchus as being Chinese. Ironically, Kangxi ruled China better than most Han emperors. He himself accepted Han culture and made significant contributions to it. He commissioned the Kangxi Dictionary, which is still regarded as the gold standard in the research of the Chinese (Han) language. With the help of Jesuit priests, he made the first map of China based on actual surveys. Kangxi learned from the shortcomings of the Ming emperors of the previous dynasty. He realised that the welfare of the people was paramount if the country was to grow and prosper. One of his policies was to stop the official takeover of people's lands and to grant a six-year tax exemption to farmers who cultivated virgin land. Taxes in general were reduced, corruption controlled and official excesses curtailed. The annual palace expenditure was slashed to a fraction of what it was in the late Ming dynasty. The palace staff, which numbered 100,000 in the late Ming dynasty, was trimmed down to only 500. The Treasury enjoyed a surplus, increasing from half-a-million taels of silver in 1671 to 41 million taels by 1694.

Militarily, Kangxi was equally effective. He put down a rebellion led by three Han warlords in the south and also regained Taiwan. On the northern front, he repelled repeated invasions by Czarist Russia. The long campaign against Russia culminated in the Treaty of Nerchinsk in 1689, where a large area of Siberia, north-east of Manchuria, fronting the Sea of Japan with Vladivostok as the southernmost port, and the adjacent Kurile Islands, officially became Chinese territory. The Siberian-Manchurian border was moved to the north, passing along the Outer Hsing-an Mountains (Stanovoy Range) to the sea. In return, Russia retained control of Nerchinsk and was given more than 240,000 square kilometres of undecided territory. Kangxi was left free to quell the uprising of Mongolian leader Galdan, and he extended his control to Outer Mongolia. Tibet once again became a Chinese protectorate. However, the subjugation of the Uighurs in the province of Xinjiang was not completely successful until the reign of Qianlong.

Yongzheng: The Institutor of Internal Reform

Yongzheng inherited the throne from his father, Kangxi, in 1723 and ruled for 13 years. A hardworking emperor, he directed his energy mainly to internal affairs. He improved the taxation system by eliminating corruption at the level of local officials and by placing tax collection directly under central control. He made taxation uniform and allowed no exception for officials and aristocrats.

He also abolished the caste system, which still existed in some provinces. A Bureau of Military Affairs was set up to consolidate all the Manchurian military groups known as "Banners" directly under the emperor's control so that the rise of warlords would be prevented.

MANCHURIAN MILITARY BANNERS

The military success of the Manchus may be largely attributed to their "Banner System". Eight "Banners" were set up, each of which would draw military manpower when needed from the colonies it administered. The colonies were occupied by Manchu settlers who farmed the land in peacetime and provided logistic support in war. Later, a similar system called the Green Corps was set up for the Hans. There was never any mixing between the Manchu Banners and the Green Corps.

Qianlong: The Emperor at the Turning Point

Qianlong became emperor in 1735 and ruled for 60 years. During the preceding two reigns, economic development had reached new heights. Agriculture flourished and food was plentiful, especially with the introduction of potato and corn into the country. The handicraft industry progressed rapidly. Exports of cotton and silk textiles, ceramics and tea to Europe and elsewhere brought in ever-increasing revenue.

This economic momentum benefited Qianlong's reign. One might say that Qianlong took over the throne at the right time and that he simply cruised along comfortably and effortlessly. He did consolidate the control of Xinjiang and Tibet and put down a rebellion in Sichuan. One notable cultural contribution he made was to commission the edition and compilation of a catalogue listing all available, reputable Chinese books in four categories. Known as *The Complete Literary Works in Four Categories* (四库全书), it references more than 36,000 volumes, resulting from the combined effort of 160 editors.

The later part of Qianlong's rule was characterised by complacency. He started to seek personal enjoyment. He made many trips to the south for pleasure and left behind a trail of tales concerning his romantic diversions. He also ordered the construction of four gigantic parks and many summer retreats at great expense. He held firm to his myopic view that China was leading the world and had nothing to learn from others. His ignorance of world events would cost China dearly.

The Decline of the Qing Empire

After the reign of Qianlong, there was a succession of six emperors from 1796 to 1911, continuing the downhill course of the empire. The country was beset by frequent insurgencies from within and repeated exploitations and invasions from without until it finally fell into a moribund state. The question here is how such an ill fate came to befall a nation once considered the wealthiest, most inventive, and most technologically advanced in the world.

The causes of the decline of China are multifarious. The imperial or civil service examination system, which had been established in the sixth century, had outlived its usefulness. It had been a good way to recruit talent for the government in ancient times but became ridiculously archaic after more than 12 centuries. The examination syllabus had remained restricted to literature. The best brains in the country were wasted in the study of outdated ancient classics in neglect of science and technology. Furthermore, examination officials were often corrupt, and the number of successful candidates was limited. Intelligent scholars would waste their entire lives trying repeatedly to pass the examination when they could have contributed significantly to society in other ways. It was not unusual to have near-senile candidates in their 70s and 80s struggling in the examination hall. Nevertheless, the lure to participate in the examination was irresistible, as it was the only way for scholars without other skills to achieve wealth and fame. By the time the Qing government came to realise the need to revamp the examination system, it was already too late; the end of the dynasty was imminent.

Another reason for the downfall of imperial China is the closed mentality of the people, especially those in power. Centuries of self-indoctrination had convinced the Chinese that they were without equal in the world. China had all it needed and there was no reason to look elsewhere or learn from others. Foreigners were looked upon as inferior; cultural and commercial exchanges with them were to be discouraged or prohibited. The Chinese, deluded by their past glory, were not aware that Europe with its industrial revolution had far

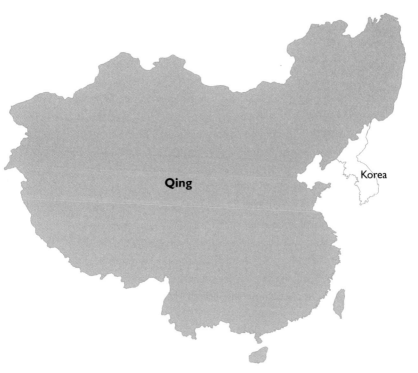

Qing

Korea

outdistanced them. Japan was able to see more clearly as it embarked on reforms in 1867 with the Meiji Restoration. In less than 50 years, Japan transformed itself into a modern nation and became a power to be reckoned with.

As if the heavy baggage of the cultural past were not enough, China also had the misfortune of having an empress dowager by the name of Cixi (慈禧) to hasten its decline. Cixi was the widow of Emperor Xianfeng (咸丰), who had ruled from 1851 to 1861. She assumed the regency for her son, the infant emperor Tongzhi (同治), from 1862 to 1874. When Tongzhi died in 1874, Cixi chose her three-year-old nephew, Guangxu (光绪), to be his successor and continued to act as the regent. For 46 years, until her death in 1908, she was *de facto* ruler of China "behind the curtain", a term referring to the fact that she attended imperial audiences behind a curtain.

After Emperor Guangxu reached adulthood, he could see that the country needed modernisation. In 1898, he took the advice of reformists such as Kang Youwei (康有为), Liang Qichao (梁启超) and Tan Sitong (谭嗣同) and tried to implement widespread reform measures. The movement lasted 103 days before it was aborted by Cixi and her conservative officials. The reformists sought the support of General Yuan Shikai (袁世凱), commander of the New Army, but were betrayed by him. Cixi placed the emperor under house arrest and started a purge. Kang and Liang escaped but Tan refused to flee and died a martyr. Five other reformists were also executed. It was doubtful whether Guangxu's belated reform would have turned the tide for China, but the last chance for the Qing dynasty to survive was destroyed by Cixi.

THE EMPRESS BEHIND THE THRONE

The empress dowager Cixi excelled in manipulation and intrigue. A selfish and cruel woman, she was concerned mainly with her position and power. She spent the funds meant for the modernisation of the Chinese navy on the Summer Palace, and is supposed to have delayed the building of railways in China by 23 years simply because she did not like trains.

The First Opium War (1840 – 1842)

In 1599, the British East India Company was formed to break the Dutch monopoly of the spice trade in the East Indies. It later grew to be more than just a trading company as it embarked on territorial occupation in India. By the mid nineteenth century, Britain had occupied the whole of India. It had earlier taken control of Singapore in 1819, Burma (Myanmar) in 1824 and Afghanistan in 1838.

The East India Company's trade with China constantly showed a deficit in the early years because British goods were not in much demand in China. In 1757, Britain occupied Bengal and began opium cultivation on a large scale. Large quantities of opium were then exported to China, mainly through armed smuggling, as foreigners were not allowed to trade freely in China. The opium export to China increased by leaps and bounds. In short order, the trade balance was reversed and China sank into great financial difficulty. Opium addiction became widespread and permeated all levels of society, including the ranks of high officials and military officers.

The sale of opium was banned by the Chinese government as early as 1729, but enforcement was not effective. In 1838, Lin Zexu (林则徐) was appointed Imperial Commissioner by Emperor Daoguang (道光) with the specific task of putting an end to opium smuggling in Guangzhou (广州). Lin Zexu took the no-nonsense approach. He confiscated all the opium he could find and destroyed it. Smugglers and traders of opium were arrested and punished.

Charles Elliot, British Chief Superintendent of Trade in China, advised the British government to intervene. In 1840, the British navy began to attack Chinese ports from Guangzhou in the south to Tianjin (天津) in the north. Superior British weaponry made the war mostly one-sided. Finally in 1842, the British took Shanghai (上海) and Zhenjiang (镇江) and sailed their gunboats up the Yangzi River to Nanjing. The Chinese government was brought to its knees and forced to sign the Treaty of Nanking (Nanjing).

THE WESTERN WOLF PACK

The outcome of the First Opium War exposed China's weaknesses and a whole pack of Western nations moved in for the spoils. American merchants had been smuggling opium into China from Turkey for some time and the United States of America began to demand the same trading concessions granted by to the British in the Treaty of Nanking. France, Portugal, Belgium, Sweden, Norway, Holland, Spain, Germany and Denmark were not far behind. All were given what they demanded. Portugal seized the opportunity to officially take over Macau as a colony while Russia occupied a large part of Manchuria and the Ili area west of Xinjiang.

The Treaty of Nanking specified the cession of Hong Kong and the opening of five ports to British merchants for trade with absolute freedom of activities, and a fixed tariff on imports and exports. Britain was granted a hefty war indemnity said to be equal to a third of a year's revenue for the Chinese government. A supplementary treaty gave British consuls the right to try their own people. It also gave Britain the automatic right to any concession that China might grant to a third power in the future.

The Taiping Rebellion (1851 – 1864)

After the First Opium War, Chinese peasants faced increasingly harder times due to the actions of corrupt officials and natural disasters. Rebellions would sporadically break out, leading up to the Taiping Rebellion, which almost toppled the Qing dynasty.

Hong Xiuquan (洪秀全), born in 1814, was a village schoolteacher who had been greatly affected by his failures to pass the imperial examination. He became a Christian after a missionary gave him a booklet about God sending His Son, Jesus Christ, to Earth to atone for the sins of mankind. Hong and some friends of a similar background started to spread the religion in the southern province of Guangxi (广西). Hong wrote several books expounding his concept of God's teachings. He also claimed to be God's second son, sent to Earth to help mankind, and his following grew rapidly in strength.

In 1850, Hong organised his followers into an army and proclaimed the birth of the Heavenly Kingdom of Universal Peace, known in Chinese as *Taiping Tienguo* (太平天国), *tai ping* meaning "universal peace". He called himself the Heavenly King and made the other five leaders of the movement subsidiary kings. In the same year, two Qing armies sent to quell the rebellion were defeated.

Boosted by initial military success, the Taiping army marched northwards, gathering strength along the way as more and more peasants joined up. In less than three years, Hong Xiuquan managed to occupy a big chunk of land along the Yangzi River. He took Nanjing and made it the capital. At the height of its success, the Taiping army even took Tianjin, forcing the Qing emperor to leave Beijing temporarily for safety.

However, the decline of the Taiping kingdom was soon imminent. Comfortable in Nanjing, the leaders started to enjoy luxurious lives. Hong himself lost his impetus and lived like a traditional Chinese emperor, filling his new palace with numerous concubines. The leaders began to fight among themselves. Eventually, Qing general Zeng Guofan (曾国藩) managed to crush the Taiping army, and the Heavenly Kingdom came to an end in 1864.

The Second Opium War (1856 – 1860)

The Second Opium War started when the Qing government was still in the midst of putting down with the Taiping Rebellion. Not content with the trade concessions they had gained through the Treaty of Nanking, Britain and France began to demand that more ports and several inland cities be opened and made available for direct trade. They also insisted that the Qing government make moves to legalise the opium trade and abolish tariffs.

THE PILLAGING AND DESTRUCTION OF THE OLD SUMMER PALACE

The most notorious act of the Anglo-French army when they invaded Beijing in 1860 during the Second Opium War was the plundering and burning of the Old Summer Palace, also known as Yuan Ming Park (圓明园). The building of Yuan Ming Park in the suburb of Beijing had been started by Emperor Qianlong. It was expanded and renovated over the next 150 years. Reputed to be the best park in the world, it covered 35 square kilometres with a built-up area of 160,000 square metres, comprising 140 buildings and more than 100 scenic spots. The buildings included palaces that housed an enormous amount of invaluable rare books, literary works and art treasures. All the treasures were taken or destroyed by the British and French armies. They even fought among themselves over the loot. To destroy evidence of their plundering, they set fire to the park. It took three days and nights to burn it to the ground. Tourists may still visit the ruins in Beijing.

To emphasise the point, British gunboats attacked Guangzhou in 1856. The following year, Britain and France jointly invaded and occupied Guangzhou. They attacked Tianjin in 1858 and forced the Qing government to sign the Treaty of Tianjin to accede to their demands. In 1859, Britain and France again demanded a revision of the treaties. They attacked Dagu Fortress near Tianjin but suffered heavy casualties. This prompted them to assemble a navy of 200 ships and an invasion force 25,000 strong. They subsequently occupied Dagu and Tianjin and entered Beijing.

These foreign incursions forced the Chinese government to sign the Treaty of Peking (Beijing) in 1860, which granted Britain and France more privileges and payment of war indemnities.

The Division of China

At the end of the Second Opium War, imperial China was practically in its death throes. In 1858, Russia demanded the ratification of the territories it had earlier occupied in the north-east and north-west of China. The total area taken by Russia amounted to 1.44 million square kilometres. Japan invaded Taiwan in 1874 and Britain intruded into Tibet that same year. Both obtained further privileges and monetary compensations in return for their withdrawal. In 1883, France invaded northern Vietnam and attacked Taiwan and the ports of the provinces of Fujian (福建) and Zhejiang (浙江). Even though France lost badly in the land war in Vietnam, the inept Chinese government ceded over their territories in Vietnam and gave many privileges to the French.

In 1894, Japan started an undeclared war and invaded Korea, which was then a Chinese protectorate. China sent an army to Korea to help. Japan won the battle at Pyongyang and destroyed the Chinese North Sea Fleet in the Yellow Sea. It then proceeded to invade China's north-east (Manchuria). The outcome was a treaty signed in Japan that saw China giving up its influence in Korea and ceding Taiwan to Japan. Japan was given free access to several inner China cities with the right to set up factories. In addition, Japan obtained a war indemnity equal to three years of the revenue of the Chinese government. As a result, China had to borrow heavily from other countries in order to meet its obligations as outlined in the treaty.

Russia, France, Britain, Germany and Japan then openly divided China into individual spheres of influence. China was forced to allow 14 "treaty ports" to come under the rule of foreign consuls. The country had in essence become a semi-colony. The United States of America was busy fighting Spain over Cuba and the Philippines, and missed this round in the division of spoils. Nevertheless, it later forced an "open-door policy" on China to protect its trade benefits.

The Boxer Uprising and the Eight-Nation Coalition Army (1900)

Sporadic Christian missionary activities in China had begun as early as the seventh century during the Tang dynasty. By the seventeenth century, the number of missionaries working to spread their faith within the boundaries of the country had grown considerably. Nonetheless, their activities were restricted by the Qing government until the 1840s when the First Opium War and the eventual defeat of China changed that circumstance. The Qing government was subsequently forced to allow churches to be built in any location. By the end of the nineteenth century, there were 3,300 missionaries in China and the number of converts exceeded 800,000.

Some of the missionaries did not limit their work to religion. The churches sometimes acquired landed properties from the Chinese people by force. They also engaged in business and money-lending and often interfered with the law, protecting local Christians who had committed crimes. Some of the missionaries worked as military spies, collecting intelligence for Western countries and even acting as guides in some invasions.

In 1898, missionaries and local Christians in Shandong (山东) province forcibly took over a Daoist temple and built a church in its place. This led to a riot against the missionaries. The situation escalated when a group known as the "boxers" joined in the unrest, and anti-missionary violence flared up in other provinces. Foreign legations were attacked, and foreigners were killed indiscriminately. The Qing government at first tried to quell the insurgency, which has come to be known as The Boxer Uprising. Later, however, with the approval of Empress Dowager Cixi, the boxers were recruited into the army.

THE ORIGINS OF THE BOXERS

The so-called "boxers" were originally anti-Manchu secret society members loyal to the deposed Ming dynasty. At the end of the nineteenth century, they organised themselves into a sect known as The Righteous Harmonious League (义和团) with a new pupose: to save the nation. They practised Chinese martial arts and claimed to be invulnerable to bullets, knives and spears.

In retaliation to the violence done against their countrymen, an eight-nation coalition army formed by Britain, America, Russia, France, Germany, Japan, Italy and Austria invaded Tianjin and Beijing in 1900, forcing Cixi and the emperor to flee. In Beijing, the foreign troops killed and looted. The outcome was a treaty in which China dismantled its defence installations from Beijing to Tianjin and allowed foreign troops to be stationed from Beijing to the coast. China was to pay a war indemnity equal to five years of state income. The payment of the sum, with interest, would take 40 years to clear. Some of the money received by the United States of America was later converted into scholarships for Chinese students.

THE REPUBLIC OF CHINA (1912)

The 1911 Revolution

In November 1908, Emperor Guangxu died, and less than 24 hours later, Empress Dowager Cixi also passed away. Before she died, she chose Puyi (溥仪), a prince, to be the next emperor. Puyi, whose reign name was Xuantong (宣统), was the "Last Emperor". He would eventually become a common gardener under the Communist regime.

Sun Zhongshan (孙中山), also known as Sun Yixian (孙逸仙) or Sun Yatsen, was born in 1866. As a youngster, he went to live with his brother in Honolulu and attended a Christian school. From 1883 to 1892, he studied medicine in Guangzhou and later in Hong Kong. He practised medicine for a while after his graduation but soon decided that curing the nation was more important than curing individuals. In 1893, he formed the Association for the Rise of China (兴中会), a revolutionary party. He tried at first to push for reforms without resorting to armed revolution. In 1894, he presented a memorial to Viceroy Li Hongzhang (李鸿章) and unsuccessfully sought an audience with him. From 1895 to 1911, he planned or led ten uprisings against the Qing government. One strategy the revolutionaries adopted was to infiltrate the new Qing army to try to persuade some of the troops to defect to their side. None of these uprisings succeded and Sun Zhongshan suffered the loss of many of his close associates and party members. After a defeat, he would escape overseas to solicit financial support from overseas Chinese.

In 1905, Sun Zhongshan held a party meeting in Japan to unite all the revolutionary groups in China. The name of the party was changed to Alliance (同盟会). Sun also declared his Three Principles of the People (三民主义), namely, (People's) Nationalism, People's Rights and People's Welfare, in some ways similar to American president Abraham Lincoln's "government of the people, by the people and for the people". The Alliance was later renamed the Nationalist Party of China, the Zhongguo Guomindang (中国国民党),

commonly known as the Kuomintang, and the party has held the Three Principles sacrosanct until today.

On 10 October 1911, Nationalist Party members staged a successful uprising in Wuchang (武昌) with the help of some Qing troops who had defected. Within a short time, 14 provinces declared their independence and seceded from the Qing government. On 1 January 1912, Sun Zhongshan took office as elected *pro tem* president and declared the founding of the Republic of China with the capital situated in Nanjing. However, the government of the Republic was extremely vulnerable and presided over a fragmented and disorganised country.

Sun Zhongshan tried to lure Qing General Yuan Shikai, who had betrayed the reformists in 1898 and now commanded a large new army in Beijing, to the side of the Republic by offering him the office of *pro tem* president. Yuan, backed by Western powers, double-crossed both the Qing court in Beijing and the Republic government in Nanjing. He forced Puyi to vacate the throne and assumed the office of President of the Republic of China. To gain Japanese backing, he signed the infamous Treaty of Twenty-one Concessions, granting Japan extensive rights in China's north-east. In 1915, Yuan went a step further and restored the imperial system with himself as the emperor. He only stepped down in March 1916 because of widespread opposition. When he died a few months later, chaos ensued as various warlords, backed by Western powers, carved up China.

The May Fourth Movement of 1919

The May Fourth Movement of 1919 marks the intellectual awakening of China. Years of pent-up national frustration and a feeling of doom culminated in the intense desire of the educated elite to seek national salvation.

The groundwork for the Movement was laid by a number of intellectuals, mostly gathered at the Peking (Beijing) University. Cai Yuanpei (蔡元培), a Nationalist Party member, became the Chancellor of the University in 1917. He was a scholar who had passed the imperial examination under the Qing government and later obtained a Ph.D in Germany. He appointed Chen Duxiu (陈独秀) as Dean of Arts. Chen was also a successful candidate in the imperial examination, and he subsequently studied in Japan and France. He had published a monthly magazine called *New Youth* since 1915. It served as a forum for intellectuals to air their views. The common theme was that China had to discard outdated aspects of Confucian teaching, change the prevailing closed mentality, rid society of archaic and corrupt practices, and move towards reform and progress. Lu Xun (鲁迅), a former medical student, was one of the most effective writers. His pungent essays and satirical short novels, which exposed undesirable traditional Chinese codes of ethics and a self-deceiving mentality, strongly influenced the youths of that era. Li Dazhao (李大钊), who was on the editorial board of the magazine, wrote about Marxism and the Soviet Revolution. Hu Shih (胡适), who had a Ph.D from Columbia, was the strongest advocate of replacing the archaic classic style of the Chinese language with the plain vernacular form. The intellectual revolution against the shackles of traditional thinking soon spread to other parts of China.

The First World War ended in 1918 with the defeat of Germany and Austria. China had contributed a battalion to the war and was supposed to have been on the winning side. However, via the Versailles Settlement, German privileges and occupied territories in the province of Shandong were given to Japan. On 4 May 1919, thousands of students took to the streets of Beijing to protest against the unfair treaty. Students in other major cities followed suit and staged demonstrations to protest foreign privileges. When warlords arrested some of the students, factory workers in many cities went on strike to support the movement. The Communists were quick to organise the workers into a formidable force. The following few years saw widespread strikes by workers against rapacious warlords and foreign interests.

THE DRIVE TO REFORM

The objective of the May Fourth Movement was twofold. Externally, the Chinese people demanded an end to the unfair treaties and special rights that Western powers and Japan had forced on China for decades. Internally, the educated pushed for intellectual renewal and a departure from the undesirable aspects of traditional culture.

The Fragile Unification

The period between 1916 and 1928 marked the warlord era in China. The country was fragmented into a number of essentially autonomous regions, each controlled by a warlord, who was usually backed by a foreign power. The Republic government in Nanjing under the Nationalist Party had only limited influence. Sun Zhongshan attempted to subdue the warlords but was unable to make much headway. In the meantime, the Communists, beginning with Li Dazhao in Shanghai, had begun to organise themselves in various cities, leading up to the official founding of the Chinese Communist Party in 1921.

Unable to unify China further, Sun Zhongshan eagerly accepted assistance and advice from the Soviet Union. In the first national congress of the Nationalist Party in 1924, Sun reorganised his party along the Soviet line. He allowed Communists to join the Nationalist Party as individuals despite objections from rightists. Comintern, the international organisation of communist parties, decided in January 1923 that it would be advantageous for Chinese Communists to cooperate with and remain within the Nationalist Party.

Sun Zhongshan announced his new policy of linking with the Soviet Union and the Chinese Communists, and of helping farmers and workers. Communist cells within the Nationalist Party became increasingly active and teamed up with the left wing of the Party. Sun Zhongshan also sent his right-hand man, Jiang Jieshi (蒋介石), more familiar to some as Chiang Kaishek, to study in Russia. He came back four months later with Russian advisors and was appointed the first Commandant of the Whampoa Military Academy in 1924. Zhou Enlai (周恩来), who would later become a Communist leader, was appointed Deputy Head of Political Education at the Academy. It was during this period that the Nationalists and the Communists became strange bedfellows.

Sun Zhongshan died of illness in 1925, and Jiang Jieshi became the leader of the Nationalist Party. By 1926, the Whampoa Military Academy under Jiang had produced several thousand officers. They formed the core of the Nationalist army. Jiang then began the Northern Expedition, successfully defeating and assimilating warlord armies along the way. The expedition was spearheaded by an independent unit under Ye Ting (叶挺), who would later become a famous Communist general.

There were three powerful warlords in the north who were in Jiang's way. He defeated two of them but had to face Zhang Zuolin (张作霖), who occupied north-east China (Manchuria) and held a large army. Zhang had initially been backed by the Japanese but the alliance disintegrated and he was assassinated by the Japanese in 1928. The North-Eastern Army then came under the command of his 28-year-old son, Zhang Xueliang (张学良), who subsequently declared allegiance to the Nationalist government.

China thus managed to achieve some semblance of unification although most warlords submitted only nominally. The position and influence of a warlord depended solely on his army. Without his military base, a warlord would be eliminated. Thus, all the warlords continued to command their individual armies although they were supposed to obey the central government.

The Long March

Jiang Jieshi carried out a bloody purge of the Communists when he entered Shanghai during the Northern Expedition. The left wing of the Nationalist Party subsequently rejoined the right wing and the Communists fled to the mountainous Jiangxi (江西) province. They had been unable to carry out effectively the instructions from Comintern, issued in May 1927, on land reform, the control of the Nationalist Party and the formation of a reliable army with recruits from Communist Party members, workers and the farmers.

Between 1931 and 1934, the Nationalist army launched repeated attacks on Communist strongholds in Jiangxi and the neighbouring provinces but suffered defeats on several occasions. Eventually, the Communist Red Army had to retreat and escape to the south and finally to the northwest, reaching Yan'an (延安) in the province of Shaanxi (陕西). That was the famous "Long March" of more than 9,600 kilometres.

It was during the March that Mao Zedong (毛泽东) rose to become the undisputed leader of the Chinese Communist Party. It was said that only some 30,000 men out of the original 90,000 survived the Long March. Many were killed while others died of starvation, disease and exposure. Those were the darkest hours for the Chinese Communists.

The Legacy of Sun Zhongshan

Sun Zhongshan's doctrine of the Three Principles of the People was interpreted in different ways by Nationalists and Communists. Sun himself also redefined his doctrine.

"Nationalism" had originally meant driving away the Manchus but was later interpreted as resisting exploitative foreign powers. "People's Rights" was widely taken to mean democracy, but Sun had said that to achieve eventual democracy, the country needed to undergo a period of one-party rule under the Nationalist Party. Jiang Jieshi claimed to be a faithful follower of Sun's teachings. He justified his actions in the purge of the Communists as necessary because they were subverting the Nationalist Party and attempting to take it over. On the other hand, the Chinese Communists accused Jiang Jieshi of betraying Sun Zhongshan's policy. After all, Sun did advocate working with the Soviet Union and the Chinese Communists. "People's Welfare" was taken to mean protecting the people against capitalists and would be in line with communism.

Even within Sun Zhongshan's family, there was no agreement on Sun's intended policy. Sun's son by his first wife, Sun Ke (孙科), served under Jiang Jieshi, whereas Sun's second wife, Song Qingling (宋庆龄), who was the sister of Madame Jiang Jieshi, went over to the Communist side.

The Japanese Invasion of North-East China

The overt Japanese invasion of China began in 1931. Prior to that time, Japan had had a military presence in the north-east and controlled the railway lines. The large Japanese army stationed there, known as the Kwantung Army, had drawn up a plan to take over the entire north-east.

On the fateful night of 18 September, some Japanese soldiers set off an explosion in the Japanese-controlled South Manchurian railway near a Chinese army camp. The plan was to lure the Chinese soldiers out of the camp and blame the explosion on them. When no Chinese soldiers appeared, the Japanese troops attacked the camp anyway and started an undeclared war. Chinese troops in the north-east had already been ordered by the central government not to engage the Japanese under any circumstances. The North-Eastern Army under Zhang Xueliang withdrew without a fight, as ordered by Jiang Jieshi. Japan proceeded to occupy the three provinces in the north-east, commonly known as Manchuria. A puppet government called Manchukuo was set up by the Japanese with the last Qing emperor, Puyi, as the head.

As the sequel to the invasion of the north-east, Japan attacked Shanghai on 28 January 1932. Japan boasted it would take Shanghai in four days and the whole of China in three months. This time, the Chinese 19th Route Army put up a stubborn fight. In March, the League of Nations, Britain and the United

States of America intervened and brought about a ceasefire and withdrawal of Japanese troops.

The Xi'an Incident

Japan actively invaded China while Jiang Jieshi was busy fighting the Communists. The policy Jiang adopted during this time called for the military to give way to Japan while concentrating on destroying the Communists.

Jiang felt that an all-out war with Japan at this juncture would certainly result in defeat for the Chinese and the total subjugation of a disunited China. There was no foreign aid in sight except possibly from Russia, a longtime enemy of Japan. It would not be in Russian interests if Japan were to successfully conquer China. Jiang wanted to gain a firm control of the entire country before turning on Japan, and he had hoped, unrealistically, that by not confronting Japan at this time, it would have no further excuse to invade China.

Jiang ordered the North-Eastern Army under Zhang Xueliang to withdraw from the north-east and to proceed to Xi'an to mop up what was left of the Red Army after the Long March. The 17th Route Army, commanded by Yang Hucheng (杨虎城), had been stationed in the area and was ordered to join the anti-Communist campaign, Jiang having apparently overlooked the fact that General Yang was known to be left-leaning. Although Zhang's army and the 17th Route Army together greatly outnumbered the Red Army, the Communists won several battles. Neither Zhang nor Yang was enthusiastic about the mission and, as the campaign stagnated, a virtual ceasefire came into effect. In the meantime, the Communists tried actively to influence Zhang and Yang. In April 1936, a non-aggression pact was secretly reached between the Communists and Zhang and Yang as they agreed to form a united front to fight the Japanese.

Jiang Jieshi's policy of yielding to Japan while carrying on a civil war drew widespread criticism from the people. The Communists spared no effort in condemning Jiang through intense propaganda, which penetrated all layers of society.

Young General Zhang Xueliang, a patriot, seethed with anger when his countrymen labelled him the "unresisting general" for the ease with which he had handed over his home in the north-east to the Japanese. He was eager to fight the Japanese and clear his name. He also suspected, not without justification, that Jiang was trying to kill two birds with one stone by pitching his not-so-loyal army against the Communists. When Jiang issued a very stern order warning Zhang and Yang to resume the anti-Communist campaign earnestly, the stage was set for the Xi'an drama.

UNEVENLY MATCHED OPPONENTS

There was a great disparity in military training and equipment between China and Japan. Chinese soldiers were poorly trained and equipped. The Japanese army was a modern one, capable of taking on any Western nation. Japan had 330 tanks while China had none. Japan had 2,700 warplanes and China had only 314. A great proportion of the Chinese army was, in fact, in the hands of the warlords, who would not be too keen to risk losing their military strength.

On 12 December 1936, when Jiang Jieshi and some high-ranking generals were in Xi'an for a conference, they were arrested by Zhang and Yang. Jiang was finally released after he promised to unite with the Communists to fight the Japanese. Ironically, the Communists helped to spare their archenemy Jiang's life and negotiate a peaceful settlement. Zhou Enlai, one of the Communist leaders, played an active part in the affair. Apparently, if Jiang were killed, there would be an all-out civil war, which would provide Japan with a golden opportunity to conquer China with ease. The situation would also spell doom for the Chinese Communists, who needed time to recuperate.

After his release, Jiang went back to Nanjing. Zhang accompanied him to the capital to face punishment and was placed under house arrest for life. By the end of the subsequent eight-year Sino-Japanese War, the Red Army had grown 30 times in military strength. The Xi'an incident had changed the course of Chinese history.

The Sino-Japanese War

The Sino-Japanese War began on 7 July 1937 at the Marco Polo Bridge (芦沟桥) near Beijing. Japanese troops were carrying out a military exercise around the bridge. On the pretext of searching for a missing soldier, Japanese troops tried to enter nearby Wanping City (宛平). A battle broke out as the defenders stood their ground.

On 17 July, Jiang Jieshi declared China's decision to defend the country should Japan persist with its aggression, and he warned the nation that it would be a fight to the end with no turning back. Japan paid no heed to Jiang's warning and went on to attack and occupy Beijing and Tianjing. All-out war became unavoidable. The Chinese Communists and all the warlords rallied around Jiang and acknowledged him as leader. As it turned out, the united front was not so solid, and Jiang often had difficulty getting his orders followed. The war would last eight years until the end of the Second World War in 1945. According to Chinese records, Chinese military and civilian casualties were a whopping 35 million. The country was badly destroyed; numerous cities became unfit for habitation. The economy was totally ruined, and inflation became uncontrollable. In the end, China received no compensation from Japan. The real winners of the Sino-Japanese War were the Soviet Union and the Chinese Communists.

The Battle of Shanghai and the Nanjing Massacre

After occupying Beijing, Japanese troops continued to invade northern China and won several battles with relative ease. On 13 August 1937, a large Japanese army supported by the air force and warships attacked Shanghai, hoping to take the city within a few days. China decided to make a stand there and amassed several divisions for the battle. Chinese troops suffered heavy casualties but continued to fight tenaciously. The bloody battle lasted three months before what was left of the Chinese defenders pulled out. Eight hundred soldiers of the Chinese 88th Division continued to fight from a warehouse. The heroic act was an inspiration to the Chinese, and the song *The 800 Heroes* became one of the most popular Chinese war songs of the time.

After the occupation of Shanghai, the Japanese attacked the capital at Nanjing. The capital was moved to Chongqing (重庆) in the mountainous Sichuan province to the west, and China put up an ill-planned defence of Nanjing. Japanese troops entered Nanjing and the soldiers were turned loose to kill and rape for six weeks. These barbaric acts were intended to demoralise the Chinese and break their will to resist. Three hundred thousand Chinese were massacred in what is referred to today as the "Rape of Nanjing".

The One-Sided War

The Sino-Japanese War was one-sided to begin with. The poorly trained

Chinese soldiers were desperately short of modern weapons and equipment. Furthermore, although the warlords' armies, the Communist 8th Route Army (the reorganised Red Army) and the New 4th Army were supposed to be under a central command headed by Jiang, they would often ignore orders and fight or retreat on their own.

In the eight years, the Chinese Nationalist army lost most of the major battles in the war except those at Taierzhuang (台儿庄) and Changsha (长沙). The battle of Taierzhuang on the southern border of Shandong province took place in March 1938 and was the first major victory for China. Chinese troops under the command of General Li Zongren (李宗仁) encircled the Japanese 10th Division and in 13 days of bloody fighting inflicted some 16,000 Japanese casualties. There were tales of Chinese suicide bombers who tied explosives to their bodies and went under Japanese tanks. The other major victory was in Changsha in Hunan province in April 1942. The Chinese commander was General Xue Yue (薛岳). Japanese casualties were estimated in Chinese reports to be around 57,000. The victory was significant in that Japan had just conquered Malaya, Indonesia and the Philippines, effortlessly driving away British and American troops.

The Communist troops confined themselves to guerrilla warfare, effectively infiltrating enemy lines while avoiding frontal battles. The 8th Route Army inflicted a few hundred Japanese casualties when it ambushed a supply convoy near Fort Pingxing (平型) in Shanxi province. It scored another major victory in 1940 when 150,000 troops were mobilised in a series of attacks on Japanese forces along the Zhengtai (正太) railway near Taiyuan (太原). The heavily guarded railway was preventing the free movement of guerrillas from one side to the other, and the Red Army decided to destroy it. The battle was called the "Hundred-battalion Battle" for it was the largest fighting force assembled by the Communists up to that time. Thereafter, the Communists fought no major battle. In fact, after Russia signed a non-aggression pact with Japan in 1941, Communist anti-Japanese guerrilla activities were curtailed.

The Chinese strategy was to use the vast space of China to bog down the Japanese and buy time. Japan was initially confident it would conquer China in three months, and it did not expect that the war would go on for years. China paid the price in human lives for holding down more than a million Japanese soldiers. In the end, the Allies trivialised China's contributions in the Second

World War and secretly sold out its interests with the signing of the Yalta Agreement towards the end of the war.

The Civil War within the Sino-Japanese War

The Nationalists and the Communists formed a united front to resist Japanese invasion in 1937. The Red Army was reorganised as the 8th Route Army and assigned to the north to fight the Japanese. Communist units south of the Yangzi River later grouped to form the New 4th Army. Practically all the major frontal battles were fought by Nationalist forces while Communist troops were engaged mainly in guerrilla warfare.

Incongruously, skirmishes were common between Nationalist and Communist troops, and both sides blamed these on the other. The Nationalists claimed that when they advanced on the Japanese, they were often hindered by Communist guerrillas following in the rear and taking the land, and that when they suffered a defeat, their stragglers were captured and absorbed into Communist guerrilla units. Mao Zedong made it plain to the cadres that the Communist policy was "70 per cent expansion, 20 per cent dealing with the Kuomintang (Nationalists), and 10 percent fighting the Japanese". Indeed, Mao succeeded well in his plan. The Red Army grew tremendously in strength in the eight-year Sino-Japanese War from around 30,000 at the end of the Long March to 900,000 at the end of the war.

The success of the Communists was due in large extent to the land reform policies they instituted in the areas they occupied and their organisation of the peasants into a friendly and supportive force. The Nationalist government, on the other hand, was politically disunited and economically exhausted. They carried the burden of large-scale frontal battles with the Japanese. The welfare of the people was not a priority.

To minimise conflicts with the Communists, the Nationalist government tried to draw a line between the two camps. Communist guerrillas were told to confine themselves to the north. The Communist New 4th Army south of the Yangzi River was ordered to go north. When the order was ignored, Nationalist troops attacked the New 4th Army and captured its commander. The Nationalists wanted the New 4th Army disbanded, but the Communists responded by increasing its strength and appointing a new commander. Thereafter, the conflict between the two camps became more intense.

The War Supply Lines

When China showed no signs of giving up resistance after the loss of the capital Nanjing, Japanese troops continued to advance. The next target was Wuhan (武汉), a city by the Yangzi and gateway to Sichuan. After a few fierce battles, the Chinese withdrew from Wuhan in October 1938. Japan had hoped that the conquest of Wuhan would be the blow to bring China down on its knees, but that did not happen.

In the first few years of the Sino-Japanese War, China purchased its military supplies from Russia, transported by land through Xinjiang. A loan for the purpose was granted by Russia. Russia sold China 1,000 planes in three years and sent volunteer pilots to help out. Russia was keen to have China hold down the Japanese army and slowly whittle away its fighting power. However, in 1941, Russia negotiated a non-aggression pact with Japan and totally cut off military aid to China. Hitler's campaign in Europe was going well, and Russia was concerned that Germany and Japan might jointly invade Russia on two fronts.

Earlier, China had also been purchasing supplies from Germany and the international market. These supplies were shipped by sea and transported into China by way of Hong Kong and Guangzhou. When Japan joined the Axis forces, Germany stopped selling China arms. Japan later conquered southern China and interrupted China's sea supply line. China then had to resort to the Burma Road, the only lifeline left.

The Burma Road, constructed by the Chinese, linked Lashio in Burma (Myanmar) to Kunming in China. It was a winding and mountainous road that was difficult to negotiate. Supplies that reached Rangoon (Yangon) were shipped by rail to Lashio and transported to China on trucks. When Japan took Indochina in 1941 and Burma in 1942, all of China's lifelines were cut off. For three years, China had to rely on a trickling of American war supplies airlifted over the Himalayas from India. It was said that American aid to China in the war amounted to only one-fortieth of the aid to Britain and one-twentieth of the aid to Russia. Although China held down a million Japanese troops, it was given very low priority.

In the meantime, Japan was obtaining large amounts of supplies from Western nations. The United States of America continued to sell petroleum and steel to Japan until 1940. The embargo that was subsequently imposed provoked Japan into starting the Pacific War.

The Nanjing Puppet Government

As the Sino-Japanese War raged, Japan grew increasingly concerned about being bogged down in the vast land of China without an early victory in sight. An alternative to continuing the war was to have a new pro-Japanese, anti-Communist Chinese government formed that would submit to Japanese control.

Some leaders on the Chinese side too had become quite pessimistic about fighting a losing war with the severe shortage of military supplies. They came to believe that Japan would eventually and inevitably succeed in subjugating China. A truce with Japan under reasonable terms was considered an option. One such leader was no less than the second man in the Nationalist government and deputy leader of the Nationalist Party, Wang Jingwei (汪精卫). Wang joined the revolution under Sun Zhongshan in the early days and had remained a prominent leader in the Nationalist Party. He was known to be staunchly anti-Communist. With the help of intermediaries, Wang defected to the Japanese side in 1939 and formed a puppet government in Japanese-occupied Nanjing. Though Wang's original plan might have been to save China from total subjugation, he played into Japanese hands. He failed to rally the Chinese to his leadership and was widely condemned as a traitor. He died in Japan in 1944.

Chennault and Stilwell: Two Americans in China

Two Americans played a direct role in the Sino-Japanese War. Claire L. Chennault was revered by the Chinese as a hero and a friend in need as he had come to their aid at a critical time. However, feelings for General Joseph W. Stilwell, American-appointed Chief of Staff for China, were mixed. Many Chinese felt his biased and stubborn attitude added to unnecessary misery in China. His inept command was also blamed for causing a fiasco in the campaign to retake Japanese-occupied Burma during the Second World War.

Chennault was a captain in the U.S. Army who had been forced to retire at the age of 44, officially on grounds of his health, but unofficially quite possibly because he believed that fighter planes could intercept and destroy enemy bombers before they reached their target, a view that was ahead of its time and one with which his superiors did not agree. He was recruited by Jiang Jieshi to be the Chief of Staff for the air force in 1937 and was joined by some of his old colleagues from the U.S. Army.

Chinese fighter pilots under Chennault's command destroyed many unescorted Japanese bombers, but their planes were later outclassed by the new Japanese Mitsubishi A5Ms. In 1938, Chennault was sent to Kunming (昆明) to train Chinese pilots. After the outbreak of the Pacific War, China belatedly obtained Tomahawk II planes from the United States of America. The American Volunteer Group was formed with pilots recruited from the United States of America. Under Chennault's command, the pilots were hailed as "Flying Tigers" for their spectacular victories over the Japanese air force near Kunming and over Burma in late 1941 and early 1942.

The American Volunteer Group formally became the U.S. Army's 14th Air Force with Chennault as commander in 1942. Chennault had to battle his three superiors – Stilwell, Chief of Staff General George C. Marshall and air force commander H.H. Arnold – constantly over supplies and strategies. In the end, he was forced to retire in mid 1945 as a major general. When he left the Chinese wartime capital of Chongqing, hundreds of thousands of Chinese packed the streets for the farewell. The car carrying Chennault had its ignition turned off and the Chinese pushed it all the way to the airport.

General Joseph Stilwell was picked by U.S. Chief of Staff George Marshall to be Jiang Jieshi's Chief of Staff in the newly established China Theatre in March 1942. He had served as military attachè in the U.S. Embassy at Beijing from 1932 to 1939. He was given command of the Chinese troops sent to Burma and he took charge of the Burma campaign as Deputy Supreme Allied Commander under British Vice-Admiral Louis Mountbatten.

Nicknamed "Vinegar Joe" by the British because of his offensive attitude, Stilwell was at odds with several British generals as well as Chennault. He particularly disliked and despised Jiang Jieshi, whom he called "Peanut Head". He filed many damaging reports to the American president, Franklin D. Roosevelt, through Marshall accusing Jiang of being uncooperative, undemocratic and interested only in American aid. He also said Jiang had no ability and intention to fight the Japanese. It was said that Stilwell had wanted to take over command of the entire Chinese army.

The Chinese sustained the war against Japan on trickling American aid, which they felt Stilwell had tried to influence in an attempt to prevail over Jiang. Many also felt that Stilwell's command in the Burma campaign was inept and had led to unnecessarily heavy casualties. In the first part of the campaign,

Allied troops were apparently poorly coordinated and intelligence gathered by the British was misleading. Stilwell underestimated Japanese strength and made several strategic mistakes. When the Allied line was broken through, there was complete disarray. Tens of thousands of Chinese troops under Stilwell's command were left to seek their own escape routes, and casualties were heavy. It is said that Stilwell left his command with a small party and escaped on foot through the jungle. He emerged in India to be hailed as a hero by the American press.

The second part of the Burma campaign directed by Stilwell in northern Burma also appeared poorly planned and executed. It took Allied troops several months to take the city of Myitkyina at a loss that could hardly be offset by the gain. Stilwell blamed British troops for not obeying his orders promptly. Despite Marshall's confidence in him, Stilwell was thought by some to be incapable of handling the complications of a theatre command; he was an excellent field general but not as competent as an army commander.

Because Stilwell took the best divisions from the Chinese army to Burma and diverted air force and military supplies from China, the defence of China was left wide open. Japanese troops advanced against weak opposition and threatened Chongqing. The wartime capital was bombed mercilessly and it gained the dubious distinction of being the most-bombed city in the world.

The differences between Jiang and Stilwell intensified. The situation came to a head when Stilwell bluntly confronted Jiang and delivered to him a directive from Roosevelt asking Jiang to hand over the command of the entire Chinese army. Jiang refused and insisted that Stilwell be removed. Jiang threatened to cut Chinese-American ties if Stilwell were not recalled. Roosevelt, realising that China was still needed to pin down a huge Japanese army, recalled Stilwell and sent General Albert C. Wedemeyer to take over as Jiang's Chief of Staff in October 1944. Miraculously, the situation soon turned around. Chennault's air plan was given priority and Chinese troops were given better equipment and training. Whether consequently or coincidentally, further Japanese advances were effectively checked.

The Ramifications of the Burma Campaign

The Allied forces faced many problems in the Burma campaign. As Japan began invading South-East Asia, China saw the importance of defending Burma, for the Burma Road was its only land lifeline. However, China's offer to help defend Burma was not accepted by Britain until 10 February 1942, one day before the Japanese invasion of Burma, when Britain requested that China send troops urgently. China sent its best divisions but there was insufficient time for preparations and the proper planning of strategy. With confusion in the command, the campaign was doomed.

In the second part of the campaign, the Allies planned to recover Burma but the three Allied nations each had their own agendas. Britain was mainly interested in defending India and initially wanted China to hold down Japanese troops in Burma. It later showed reluctance to let Chinese troops in to retake Burma, and kept delaying the second part of the Burma campaign. Apparently, British Prime Minister Winston Churchill, basically an imperialist, envisaged the recovery of British colonies in Asia after the war, and did not want the colonies liberated before the war in Europe was won. China, whose main concern was re-establishing the Burma Road, now felt that the land supply line would no longer be useful as the Indian Ocean shipping route was controlled by Japan.

China favoured an all-out land and sea war. However, the Allies' strategy, strongly advocated by Churchill, assigned priority to Europe over the Pacific. China was considered least important. British and American naval forces were more urgently needed in the Mediterranean and Pacific Oceans. After a year's delay, an invasion of northern Burma was decided upon, mainly to protect the Ledo Road (later renamed Stilwell Road), which was being built as a land supply line for China from Assam in India to the Burma Road near the Chinese border. China contributed most of the land forces for the campaign and bore the brunt of the battles. North Burma was recovered with heavy losses.

The Ledo Road, built through extremely hostile terrain, was completed by American engineers near the end of the war and had been in use for less than six months when Japan surrendered. Both the Burma Road and Ledo Road are now in disrepair and all but forgotten.

The Yalta Agreement

In February 1945, when Allied victory over Germany was in sight, Roosevelt and Churchill turned their focus on Japan. They met Joseph Stalin, the Russian premier, at Yalta, a conference from which China was excluded.

In order to shorten the war in the Pacific and save American lives, Roosevelt tried to induce Russia to enter the Pacific War. Russia agreed to fight Japan within two to three months of Germany's defeat. The price Stalin set for this agreement included the return of the Kurile Islands and Southern Sakhalin (occupied by China during the Qing dynasty and later by Japan), the occupation of the Chinese warm-water ports of Darien (Dalian) and Port Arthur, control of the Chinese Eastern Railway and the Southern Manchurian Railway, and the maintenance of the status quo in Outer Mongolia (which had gained autonomy in 1921 with Russian backing).

Roosevelt and Churchill readily agreed, and China's sovereign rights in Manchuria were signed away without its knowledge. Roosevelt was in poor health at that time, and he probably wanted to see the defeat of Japan within his lifetime. Churchill, of course, was interested mainly in the recovery of British privileges and possessions in the East. China's loss was not his concern. Little did Roosevelt and Churchill know that the Yalta Agreement would not only eventually prove to be unnecessary, it would also play a significant role in contributing to the communist conquest of China.

The Russian Invasion of Manchuria

On 6 August 1945, the first American atomic bomb was dropped on Hiroshima. Stalin became concerned that Japan might suddenly surrender, depriving Russia of the opportunity to invade Manchuria and to enjoy the privileges promised in Yalta.

On the night of 8 August, Soviet troops attacked Manchuria on three fronts without a declaration of war against Japan. The second atomic bomb was dropped on Nagasaki on 9 August. Japan surrendered on 10 August. Nevertheless, Soviet forces refused to stop after Japan's surrender and pushed the invasion beyond Manchuria in an attempt to link up with the Chinese Communists. Russia occupied Manchuria until May 1946 and during that period looted Japanese industrial plants, moving all the heavy equipment to Russia. Large quantities of Japanese arms were handed to the Chinese Communists. This contributed to the eventual downfall of the Nationalist government.

The Mad Race

After the surrender of Japan, Nationalist and the Communist troops scrambled to grab the occupied territories and take over Japanese weapons. The Communists had a geographical advantage as their guerillas were already scattered over northern China. They naturally had no difficulty entering and establishing themselves in Russian-held Manchuria. By comparison, Nationalist forces, stationed mostly in western and south-western China, were not as mobile and had to be airlifted by the Americans to occupy the major Manchurian cities. However, the countryside was by then under Communist control. In subsequent battles, the Communists drove away the Nationalists with relative ease.

The Resumption of Civil War

It is probably accurate to say that the civil war between the Nationalists and the Communists never stopped during the eight-year Sino-Japanese War when the two sides were supposed to have formed a united front against a common enemy. Skirmishes and battles took place from time to time. Jiang Jieshi was the acknowledged leader of the united front, but his command did not really extend over the Communists. He was so distrustful of the Communists that he stationed a large army near Yun'an throughout the war to keep an eye on them.

Open civil war resumed after the surrender of Japan. By then, the Communists were strong enough to engage the Nationalists directly. Washington tried to mediate for peace. When the American envoy Patrick Hurley failed, President Harry S. Truman sent George C. Marshall, the American head of the Joint Chiefs of Staff, to China to broker a peaceful settlement. Jiang was told that he would not get any American aid for the civil war. Marshall succeeded in getting both sides to come to the conference table and work out mutually acceptable terms but as soon as he left, the truce was broken. Marshall returned later to arrange for another truce, which also suffered the same fate.

The Americans were perhaps rather naive at that time and did not have sufficient insight regarding the situation in China and the nature of communism. Jiang would not tolerate the Communists. Past experience had taught him not to let the camel into the Arab's tent again. The Communists obviously would not be limited to partial control of the government as their basic agenda was directed towards the entire country, if not the whole world. Peace negotiations between the two parties were clearly futile. To quote a Chinese saying, the Nationalists and the Communists simply could not blend like "water and milk"; they were like "water and fire" and could not co-exist.

Jiang Jieshi, assured by Nationalist victories in the civil war prior to mid 1947, underestimated the Communists' strength and the sagging morale of soldiers and civilians after they had endured extreme hardship for years. Nobody was enthusiastic about another war. They persevered in the Sino-Japanese War out of nationalism and patriotism. To fight one's own people was another matter. There was general national exhaustion. With the economy at a nadir, inflation rose at a runaway pace. Corruption was rampant as everyone tried to survive. The farmers and workers were hardest hit. The stage was set for the population to turn to the Communists in the quest for a better life.

The powerful Communist propaganda network moved into high gear, penetrating extensively both inside and outside the country. The Nationalist government was condemned, not unjustifiably, as corrupt, decadent, nepotistic, rapacious, undemocratic and reactionary. Any person who empathised with the Nationalists was immediately labelled as reactionary and obstinate, and fit for elimination.

The most severe Nationalist defeat in Manchuria occurred in October 1948, in which Jiang reportedly lost 470,000 of his troops due to casualties and defections. Then followed the battle of Huai-Hai (淮海) in northern China in which the Nationalists lost another 200,000 men. The die was cast. From then on, mass retreats and defections were the order of the day. The Communists crossed the Yangzi River on 21 April 1949 and conquered Nanjing three days later. The Nationalist government was forced to flee to Guangzhou (Canton) and from there to Chongqing on 13 October.

Jiang Jieshi had begun to prepare Taiwan as a refuge at the end of 1948 so when Nanjing fell, he had troops, military equipment, gold reserves and foreign currencies evacuated there. The Nationalist government moved to Taiwan in December 1949. In the meantime, the victorious Communist forces advanced from all directions in the mainland. Even before the conquest of the country was complete, Mao Zedong proclaimed the establishment of the People's Republic of China at Tiananmen on 1 October 1949.

The Japanese Invasion and the Destiny Of China

The Nationalist Party had initially been formed by progressive, selfless young men bent on national salvation. It toppled the decadent Manchu government in 1912. It tried to unify China but could not overcome the powerful warlords. The only source of outside help available was Soviet Russia. Nationalist Party leader Sun Zhongshan embarked on the policy of linking with Russia and the Chinese Communists. He allowed communists to join his party as individual members.

When Jiang Jieshi took over the leadership, he found the Nationalist Party at risk from subversion by the communist members within. He started a bloody purge, killing many communist activists. This led to a civil war that culminated in the Long March of the Chinese Communists. The Red Army at the end of the Long March was a spent force.

Then, the Japanese invasion intensified. National opinion turned against Jiang for not resisting the Japanese. The Xi'an incident forced Jiang to abandon his anti-Communist campaign and fight the Japanese. In a way, the Chinese Communists had reason to thank Japan for indirectly giving them a long breathing spell and the opportunity to revive. Japan played a critical role in changing the destiny of China.

The leaders of the Nationalist Party had originally envisaged an eventual modern, democratic country. The Party never had a chance to realise its dream, being continuously involved in one war after another. Party leader Jiang was criticised as being autocratic, corrupt and nepotistic and running a graft-ridden government. Whatever its shortcomings, however, the Nationalist Party should be credited with resisting Japanese invasion for eight years and preventing the Japanese subjugation of China.

The Chinese are a pragmatic people. It probably did not matter to most of them which party controlled the country as long as the people were taken care of and the country strengthened. The general feeling was that China was so moribund that it needed a drastic change of medicine, as prescribed by the Communists, to regain its health. Under Mao Zedong's leadership, the nation was once again unified under an effective central authority. Unfortunately, on the bumpy road to progress, mistakes such as the Great Leap Forward and the Cultural Revolution practically erased a generation of people and created a moral vacuum in a once culture-conscious nation.

One cannot help marvelling at the rapidity and the extent of recent developments in China. Like a phoenix rising from the ashes, the renewal of the nation is truly amazing. China will no doubt become technologically modern within a short span of time. Perhaps, the time has come for it to retrieve some desirable traditional values and embark on moral rearmament so that it befits a nation with 5,000 years of civilisation.

TRADITIONAL SCHOOLS OF THOUGHT

THE CONFUCIAN SCHOOL (儒家)

Confucius: The Great Teacher

Education, once the exclusive privilege of aristocrats in ancient China, became popular and accessible to commoners during the period of the Eastern Zhou dynasty. The private tutorship system produced many thinkers and philosophers. These early scholars would influence Chinese culture for centuries to come.

Confucius was born in 551 B.C. during the Spring-Autumn period in the Eastern Zhou dynasty in Qufu (曲阜) in the state of Lu (鲁), now known as the Shandong province. His actual name was Kong Qiu (孔丘) and he was respectfully referred to as Kong Zi (孔子) or Kong Fuzi (孔夫子), meaning "Master Kong". The name was Latinised by Jesuit missionaries in China as Confucius.

Confucius introduced a school of thought that would influence Chinese culture for more than 2,000 years. As a philosopher, he preached personal virtues and social order. Basically, the individual should practise *ren* (仁), which he defined differently on different occasions. On the whole, he considered filial piety and respect for elders as the foundation of *ren*. However, according to his teaching, *ren* also encompassed practically all other virtuous human qualities such as self-discipline, propriety of conduct, altruism, kindness, humility, integrity, loyalty, courage, insight, trustworthiness and such. Some simply call it "humaneness". Confucius' idea of the "gentleman" was not one of wealth or basically good behaviour but one who was culturally ideal and morally perfect.

In matters of career, Confucius felt that an individual's ascent to a position should be stepwise with tests along the way. He advised that one should concentrate on improving oneself before undertaking to manage a family. With the proven ability to manage a family in harmony, one could then attempt to administer a state. Having passed all these tests, one might then be fit to run the whole country.

When consulted on the principles of government by the head of the Qi state, Confucius simply replied in eight words, literally translated as "ruler (should be) ruler, subject (should be) subject, father (should be) father, son (should be) son". The answer reflected Confucius' idea of a strict hierarchy and obligatory personal duty in the maintenance of familial and social order. The ruler–subject and the father–son relationships should involve reciprocal obligations. The ruler must be benevolent to deserve loyalty from his ministers and subjects, who in turn must be subservient. The father should shoulder his parental responsibility to deserve filial piety from his son, who in return must have love and respect for the father. When everyone knew his rightful place and fulfilled his part, hierarchy and order would be maintained, and there would be peace and harmony in society.

Confucius was quite obsessed with proper etiquette and ritual. In these two areas, he followed strictly the canon laid down by Zhou Gong (周公), the duke of the Zhou dynasty. *The Rites of Zhou* required one to observe appropriate etiquette and ritual according to one's rank in the family and one's status in society. The Master believed that strict observance of the prescribed etiquette and ritual was essential in maintaining family and social order.

Confucius spent 13 years travelling from state to state to preach his philosophy to the various heads. The rulers were impressed but not receptive. They probably found his ideals too lofty. In the end, he returned home and devoted the rest of his life to teaching. He emphasised to his students that learning must be accompanied by thinking so as to open up new grounds. He advocated equal learning opportunities for all who wanted to learn. "Teach without discrimination," the Master advised. He taught more than 3,000 students and rated 72 of them as outstanding. The curriculum included ethics, divination, history, poetry, etiquette and music.

Confucius never held any significant position of authority and had no opportunity to implement his ideas of government. Subsequently, however, his philosophy dominated teaching in schools and thus permeated all levels of society in practically all the dynasties. The Chinese probably owe their traditional deference to seniority and authority more to Confucian doctrine than to any other factor in their cultural upbringing. Confucius died in 479 B.C. at the age of 72. His ghost has been invoked from time to time by rulers as a means to instil obedience in the governed.

Mencius: The Confucian Philosopher

The baton of mainstream Confucianism was next passed to Mencius, who had studied under Confucius' grandson. Mencius was born around 372 B.C. His name was Meng Ke (孟轲) and he was addressed as Meng Zi (孟子) or Master Meng. The name was Latinised as Mencius.

Mencius was brought up by his widowed mother. She moved three times in search of a neighbourhood conducive to the proper upbringing of her son. When Mencius played truant as a boy, she took a pair of scissors and cut up the yarn on her loom to show him that his study would suffer the same ruinous effect if disrupted. Mencius began to study diligently and never looked back. Mencius' mother is considered a role model by the Chinese.

Mencius continued to preach the basic philosophy of Confucius and emphasise the practice of *ren*. He introduced a rudimentary concept of democracy by stating that subjects were more important than the ruler and that it was justifiable to depose a tyrannical ruler. It was Mencius' belief that man was born good but that the goodness needed to be drawn out by education. He was in favour of a systematic approach to teaching and against the forced, express method, which he likened to manually stretching a young shoot to hasten its growth.

Like Confucius before him, Mencius was frustrated in his political career. The book he wrote with his disciples, *Mencius,* remained a requisite school text for 2,000 years.

Xun Zi: The Pessimistic Confucian

The next outstanding Confucian scholar was Xun Zi (荀子), born around 315 B.C. He was especially known for his view that man was born bad, and that one's character needed to be moulded by education and modified through learning to become good and creative. His belief that human nature was inherently evil was in contrast to Mencius' view. He advocated the need for laws to control human behaviour. One of his students, Han Feizi (韩非子), was apparently so strongly influenced in this respect that he later introduced the Legalist School of Thought.

The Fall and Subsequent Resurgence of Confucianism

The first emperor of China, Qin Shi Huang, who unified China in 221 B.C., was a harsh ruler. In response to criticisms by Confucian scholars, he had more than 400 of them buried alive and had practically all the pre-Qin books burnt. Confucian teachings were suppressed.

During the early Han dynasty, which succeeded the Qin dynasty, an attempt was made by scholars to salvage Confucian books. Classics hidden in the walls of houses came to light. Those that were lost for good were rewritten from memory. Confucian classics were put together and once again held sway in schools.

FORTUNE-TELLING AND SCIENCE

The practice of divination based on the classic Yi Jing (易经) or The Study of Changes, was passed down from the early Western Zhou period. Essentially, it was fortune-telling according to the interpretation of elements and phenomena in nature. The prophecies were dispensed along with certain ethical and moral concepts that agreed well with Confucianism. Inexplicably, the book is also credited with harbouring the basic concepts of everything from physics to philosophy and genetics to government. From the present viewpoint, the part to do with fortune-telling should be regarded as superstition with no scientific basis.

Confucius probably never wrote any of the books attributed to Confucianism. The Analects was compiled by his students from his views and remarks on many topics and situations. From a large number of the short, seemingly unrelated notes, subsequent scholars were able to infer and crystallise Confucius' thoughts. In the Southern Song dynasty, during the twelfth century, a scholar named Zhu Xi (朱熹) edited The Analects and split it into three parts, namely, *Analects* (论语), *Great Learning* (大学), and *Doctrine of the Mean* (中庸). These and *Mencius* (孟子) together formed *The Four Books* (四书). The remaining classics used for Confucian teaching, pertaining to poetry (诗经), divination (易经), the records of ancient rulers (尚书), rites (礼记), and the history of the Spring-Autumn period (春秋), were collectively called *The Five Jings* (五经) or *The Five Classics*. Zhu Xi's interpretation of Confucian classics was called Neo-Confucianism and was considered orthodox.

The Confucian classics edited by Zhu Xi were used for teaching in all subsequent dynasties. They formed the core syllabus for the civil service examinations. If one were to search for a reason why old China had fallen so far behind in science and technology, one would undoubtedly place the blame squarely on the obligatory study of archaic Confucian classics, almost to the exclusion of all other subjects, for two millennia. The May Fourth Movement of 1919 and Mao's Cultural Revolution finally put down the suffocating influence of Confucianism. Nevertheless, some Confucian ethics and moral concepts have stood the test of time, and the Chinese would do well not to discard them lightly.

THE DAOIST (TAOIST) SCHOOL (道家)

Lao Zi (老子) was an older contemporary of Confucius. Confucius was said to have consulted him on matters of etiquette. His name was Li Er (李耳), but he was called the Old Master (Lao Zi) either out of respect or because of his prematurely old appearance. Lao Zi grew up in a turbulent period of Chinese history when the various states constantly fought one another. This must have influenced him to advocate the philosophy in *Dao De Jing* (道德经).

Dao De Jing is a 5,000-word treatise written by Lao Zi that captures the essence of philosophical Daoism. The concepts of *Dao* and *De* are vague and difficult to put into plain words. The two words have been variously translated as "truth and virtue" and as "way and virtue".

The treatise was written in such cryptic and arcane language as to defy easy comprehension and interpretation. For instance, the first chapter was translated by Cheng Lin as:

The truth that may be told is not the everlasting Truth. The name given to a thing is not the everlasting Name.

Nothingness is used to denote the state that existed before the birth of heaven and earth. Reality is used to denote the state where the multitude of things begins to have separate existence.

Therefore, when the mind rests in the state of Nothingness, the enigma can be understood; when the mind rests in the state of Reality, the bounds can be reached.

These two states, though bearing different names, have a common origin. Both are mysterious and metaphysical. They are the most mysterious, and form the gateway to all mysteries.

The same chapter was translated by Robert Hendricks as:

As for the Way, the Way that can be spoken of is not the constant Way;

As for the name, the name that can be named is not the constant Name.

The nameless is the beginning of 10,000 things;

The named is the mother of 10,000 things.

Therefore, those constantly without desires, by this means will perceive its subtlety.

Those constantly with desires, by this means will see only that which they yearn for and seek.

Those two together emerge; they have different names yet they are called the same;

That which is more profound than the profound –

The gateway of all subtleties.

Regardless of how the *Dao De Jing* is interpreted, most scholars agree that Lao Zi was presenting a philosophical viewpoint. He felt that all things were best left to follow their natural course without human intervention. Of course, this leads to the idea that minimal government would be the best form of government. Lao Zi also believed that people should return to the original simplicity, free of desire and free of the urge to strive, untainted by knowledge. "Not doing" (无为) or non-action was Lao Zi's main point, meaning that the best policy was to avoid active intervention.

Modern man would undoubtedly consider Lao Zi's ideology simplistic and impractical. Nevertheless, Lao Zi's idea of avoiding paternalistic meddling in governing a nation was adopted by two Han emperors (179 – 140 B.C.) with considerable success. The country became prosperous, and there was peace and order. Daoism found a following in two well-known philosophers, Zhuang Zi (庄子) and Lie Zi (列子), both of the third century B.C. They carried Lao Zi's philosophy further into the arcane world. Lao Zi would probably not have occupied a prominent place in Chinese culture if philosophical Daoism were not linked through events in history to the Dao religion.

THE LEGALIST SCHOOL (法家)

Han Feizi was born at the end of the Eastern Zhou dynasty and died in 223 B.C. during the Qin dynasty. He was a student of Xun Zi's from the Confucian school. He believed that it was human nature to be innately evil and he felt that well-defined laws specifying rewards and punishments were the answer to good government. Han criticised the traditional Confucian practice of following the doctrines of ancient kings and sages that were no longer applicable in his time.

Han Feizi's classmate Li Si (李斯) served as prime minister under Emperor Qin Shi Huang and was responsible for the harsh rule of Qin. When the emperor came across two essays written by Han Feizi, he appreciated the points and recruited him. Li Si later plotted the death of Han to safeguard his own position.

THE MISCELLANEOUS SCHOOLS

Several other schools of thought asserted themselves during the Warring States period. Among the better known were Mo Zi (墨子), who was anti-war and advocated pacifism and the love of people on a broad basis, and Su Qin (苏秦), who saw war as the only means to unify the nation.

RELIGIONS

SYNCRETISM

Religious conflict was rare in the long history of China. Around 845, during the Tang dynasty, Buddhism suffered a brief official persecution at the instigation of court Daoists and Confucian bureaucrats. Many temples were demolished, and monks and nuns were ordered to return to secular life. During the Boxer Uprising in the late Qing dynasty in 1899, the Boxers attacked Christian missionaries and foreign legations, all indiscriminately identified as foreign predators. By and large, the Chinese people see no reason to quarrel over religion and are receptive to both home-grown and imported beliefs. They are able to syncretise different religions and even worship two or more religions simultaneously. To the average worshipper of Buddhism or the Dao religion, the line between the two faiths is indistinct. Buddhist and Daoist deities are often mixed together. Conversions from one religion to another are common among the Chinese. Many older Chinese Christians are converts from other religions. It is extremely common for members of the same family to have different religious faiths.

CONFUCIANISM

A religion invariably consists of two aspects: a belief in supernatural beings and a set of principles or codes related to behaviour and conduct. The supernatural part usually spells out reward for piety and retribution for sins. Confucianism in this respect is not a religion as it pertains only to principles. There is no promise of reward or threat of punishment. Although there is mention of "heaven" and "gods", they are mainly symbolic of the authority for which one should have a healthy respect. Confucius advised, "Respect the spirits and gods but keep them at a distance". The making of offerings to heaven and ancestors was a ritual practised in Confucianism that served as a reminder that one should observe the lines that separated classes and statuses, and that one should never cease to respect authorities. The concept of "heaven", long recognised before Confucius' time, was probably retained by Confucius to keep rulers in line, as the king was considered to be the "son of heaven".

DAOISM

The Dao religion or religious Daoism is the only religion indigenous to China. It owes its name to Daoism, the philosophy of Lao Zi. Although the religion and the philosophy are of the same name, the former has evolved on its own with practically no relevance to *Dao De Jing*, the philosophy of Daoism. In the course of history, Lao Zi's name was dragged into the Dao religion.

Around 142, near the end of the Han dynasty, a scholar named Zhang Daoling (张道陵) founded the Dao religion, which he proclaimed was based on Daoism. He claimed that Lao Zi revealed to him in a dream a new orthodox Daoism. He also claimed that the religious rites he taught could cure illnesses and lead to immortality. To join the religious order, one would have to contribute five pecks of rice. Hence, the religion was also known as the "five-pecks-of-rice religion". Though an obvious charlatan, Zhang was convincing enough to attract a large number of followers. The Dao religion soon spread throughout the entire country.

THE DAOIST REBEL

In the year 184, a Daoist named Zhang Jiao (张角), claiming to have a mandate from Heaven, took advantage of the chaotic situation in China to start an uprising. The rebels wore yellow turbans in battle and were thus known as "Yellow Turban Rebels". They almost toppled the Han dynasty.

Religious Daoism met strong competition from Buddhism, which became very popular during the South-North dynasty. More and more people turned to Buddhism. Around 630, Emperor Tang Taizong, who claimed to be a descendent of Lao Zi, bestowed on Lao Zi the posthumous title of Supreme Head of the Dao Religion. This gave the Dao religion a big boost and a legitimate status. The emperor himself observed both Buddhism and religious Daoism and saw no conflict between the two. Many subsequent emperors also practised both Buddhism and religious Daoism simultaneously.

Religious Daoism has through the centuries gravitated towards the practice of supernaturalism. The philosophical Daoism of Lao Zi has generally lapsed into oblivion. It is probably accurate to say that most of those who profess to be Daoists today do not know of *Dao De Jing*, let alone understand it. Early Daoist charlatans claimed to be able to concoct immortality drugs. They found ready followers in many emperors, some of whom neglected state affairs in the quest for eternal life.

As time passed, the self-styled Daoist masters also ventured into many areas of the occult such as alchemy, exorcism, divination, the promotion of the soul status of the dead, the elevation of the living to the ranks of the gods, the curing of diseases by chanting and consumption of the ashes of burnt talismans, the enhancement of the male sexual prowess through the control of orgasms and the harnessing of the female essence, and sundry other magical practices.

Today, Daoist priests deal mainly with matters related to death and spirits. They are called upon to chant at funerals or to cleanse premises of evil spirits. The god worshipped in the Dao religion is Lao Zi, but the Jade Emperor in heaven is the supreme authority. There are many other gods who have been integrated into the Daoist faith. Many of these deities were previously distinguished mortals. A popular one is Guan Yu (关羽), a general in the Three Kingdoms, admired for his courage and righteousness. Along the south-eastern coast of China and in Taiwan, fishermen and sailors worship the goddess Ma Zhu (妈祖) for protection. Ma Zhu was supposedly a fisherman's daughter while she was alive, and her spirit became the guardian of fishermen at sea. The present practice of the Dao religion is closely linked to superstitions, as it has always been.

BUDDHISM

Buddhism spread from India to China. It is probably the most popular religion in China. The founder of Buddhism was Siddhartha Gautama, who was born a prince in a small kingdom in Nepal in 563 B.C. He is generally referred to as Sakyamuni, meaning the sage of the Sakya clan, to which he belonged. He lived a life of luxury in the palace until he was 29 years old when he became aware of the inescapable human sufferings of childbirth, old age, sickness and death. He then left his wife and son to find a way to free mankind from this fate. He eventually attained enlightenment or *nirvana*, a blissful state completely free of desire. He was then known as Buddha, and his teachings formed the essence of Buddhism.

Hinduism is India's oldest religion with a history of some 3,500 years. Buddhism shares the Hindu concepts of *karma* and *samsara*. By *karma* is meant that the sum total of one's good and bad deeds in the past will determine how one will be rewarded or punished in the next life. Generally, one is condemned to worldly suffering through the never-ending cycle of birth, death and rebirth, known as *samsara* or reincarnation. Beyond these common concepts, Buddhism branched off in search of a way to help mankind escape its fate. At his enlightenment, Buddha saw through the transitory nature of all worldly things and felt that human suffering was caused by the inability to appreciate this impermanence that led to desire and craving for wealth, fame and power, and to anger from frustration. Buddha taught the Four Noble Truths; that life is suffering, that suffering comes from desire, that desire should be eliminated, and that the way to rid oneself of desire is to follow the Eightfold Path that leads to right living and thinking.

Several different traditions of Buddhism subsequently developed in India. The two main divisions are Theravada and Mahayana. Theravada or the Teaching of the Elders closely adheres to the teachings of Gautama Buddha. In Mahayana, Gautama is considered one of many Buddhas who are different manifestations of the primordial Buddha. In addition, there are Bodhisattvas (菩萨) who delay their own *nirvana* and passionately work for the good of others. There are many other schools of Buddhism, each with its own theory of how best to attain enlightenment, whether through meditation, good deeds, philosophical inquiry or a combination thereof.

Buddhism began to spread into China as early as the first century, during the reign of Han Ming Di of the Han dynasty. Since then, Mahayana has been the prevalent form of Buddhism in China. The Buddha generally worshipped is Amitabha, who resides in the Western Pure Land or Paradise, where, it is believed, deserving souls will go. The Buddha who is to come is Maitreya, called the Mi-Le Buddha in Chinese. The most popular Bodhisattva is Avalokiteshvara, translated into Chinese as Guanshiyin (观世音), or simply Guanyin (观音) to avoid the taboo of using Tang emperor Li Shimin's name, and often called the Goddess of Mercy. The Chinese translation means "one who hears the cries of the world" or "one who perceives the pleas of the world". She is believed to be a saviour who comes to the aid of those in distress. According to the belief, she will help guide people towards enlightenment before the arrival of the next Buddha.

THE INDIAN CONNECTION

Buddhist scriptures were first translated into Chinese by Indian monks as early as the Han dynasty. Fa Xian (法显), a Chinese monk, journeyed to India in 399 via the Silk Road to study and bring back Buddhist scriptures. He sailed back to China from Ceylon 15 years after he left home and reached the mainland after a perilous voyage. Two other well-known translators were Kumarajiva, an Indian monk, and Xuan Zang (玄奘), a Chinese monk who went to India during the early Tang dynasty.

Buddhism flourished in China from the South-North dynasty through the Sui and the Tang dynasties. There was a major but short-lived official suppression of the religion for political reasons around 845. Most of the time, Buddhism co-existed well and even blended with religious Daoism and Confucianism.

Buddhism branched into at least ten schools in China. One school, called *Chan* (禅), was introduced by the Indian monk Bodhidharma (达摩). It emphasised meditation and became very popular. Monasteries were set up for large groups of residential monks. Many temples accumulated assets and became self-sufficient, thus sparing monks from wandering about to beg for alms. *Chan* Buddhism later spread to Japan, where it is known as *Zen*. The Tibetan school of

Buddhism is of the Mahayana type, with elements of esoteric Hindu practices and native Tibetan magic rituals. Over the centuries, Tibetan Buddhism has counted among its devotees Kublai Khan and several Qing emperors.

Buddhism survived in China through times both good and bad in later dynasties. It was suppressed under Communist rule but has begun to become popular again. There appears to be a need for people to have faith in the spiritual world although a great deal of the practices adhered to by the common folk, as in most other religions, would be considered superstitious from a scientific point of view.

ISLAM

Islam was founded by the Prophet Muhammad in the seventh century. According to Muslim historians and Tang dynasty records, Saad ibn Abi Waqqas, a relative of the Prophet, visited China in the year 650 to invite the Tang emperor to embrace Islam. He was very well received. The actual spread of the religion into China probably came later when Arab traders arrived in large numbers by land and sea. Many of them settled down, married Chinese women, and took up Chinese names. Some of their descendants may still be identified in southern Chinese ports.

Around 757, the Tang emperor enlisted the help of an Arab army to put down a rebellion led by An Lushan, a northern army commander. Many of the Arab soldiers did not return home but instead settled in China, passing the religion on to their descendants.

There are 17.6 million Muslims among ten ethnic groups living in China. The largest group, the Hui, numbering 8.6 million people, live mainly in the western provinces and Yunnan. However, the Hui may be found in other provinces throughout China; Beijing currently boasts a population of 220,000 ethnic Hui. The Uighurs of Xinjiang province, numbering 7.2 million people, are the second largest Muslim ethnic group in China. The Qazags in the western provinces, numbering 1.1 million people, make up the third largest group.

Islam is referred to in Chinese as the Hui religion (回教) even though the Hui people make up only 50 per cent of the Muslims in the country. It is unclear exactly how the religion came to be known by this name but it could have initially been a phonetic translation of Uighur, yet another ethnic group of Muslims in China. In the Yuan dynasty, Persians, Arabs and other Middle Eastern people living in China were called "Hui Hui". Again, the root of this naming convention is not clear. Islam is also called *Qing Zhen* (清真) in Chinese. *Qing Zhen* means "purity" and "truth" and could be a translation of the word "Islam". Mosques are commonly called *Qing Zhen* temples in China.

TRANSLATING THE HOLY WORD

From the seventeenth century to the early twentieth century, there were attempts to translate selected passages and chapters of the Islamic holy book, the Koran, into Chinese. The first complete translation was done by Li Tiezheng (李铁铮) in 1927. He based his work on the Japanese and the English versions.

CHRISTIANITY

Christianity of the Nestorian form was first introduced into China via the Silk Road during the reign of Tang Taizong in the seventh century. It vanished quite completely with the decline of the Tang dynasty.

During the Yuan dynasty in the thirteenth century, the Mongol army occupied Western Asia and Eastern Europe. Christianity in Nestorian and Roman Catholic forms was brought back to China. Once again the religion died out when the Yuan dynasty ended.

In the later part of the sixteenth century, the Roman Catholic Church, the Protestant Church, and to a lesser extent, the Russian Orthodox Church, began to make their presence felt in China. This time, the Christians came to stay. The Jesuits were the leading missionaries and the most respected Jesuit priest was Matteo Ricci, an Italian. He gained the complete acceptance of the Chinese with his in-depth knowledge of Chinese culture and customs, and his tolerance of Confucianism. Some of the missionaries who came later were not as understanding, and they tended to treat traditional Chinese practices with disdain.

Nevertheless, China benefited in no small measure from the contributions of Christian missionaries to education and health care. Missionary schools, built primarily to spread Christianity, provided countless young Chinese with a chance to gain a modern education. By 1937, the year when the Sino-Japanese War began, there were 4,000 Catholic priests, brothers and nuns, and 5,700 Protestant missionary staff in the country.

Suppression of Christianity in China occurred when the country came under the Communist rule. Religious freedom has since been restored to a large extent. The present number of Christians in registered churches is said to be between ten and 14 million. The number of unregistered Christian worshippers is estimated to be between 30 and 70 million.

THE POLITICS OF RELIGION

The spread of Christianity in China was facilitated by the various unfair treaties the Western countries forced on China. As Western influence grew, some of the missionaries became more intrusive and offensive to the traditional Chinese. The trend culminated in a temporary setback for Christianity when the Boxers resorted to violence against Western missionaries and legations in 1898.

JUDAISM

Nobody is quite sure how an obscure Jewish community with a synagogue in the old city of Kaifeng (开封) in the Henan province came to be. The place is inland, far away from the coast and from Russia. The religion was probably imported by settlers, who most likely came to China via the Silk Road.

It seems that the Jewish community in Henan existed for 700 years, from the Song dynasty in the twelfth century to the Qing dynasty in the nineteenth century. There was no religious persecution or discrimination, but the number of Jews gradually declined, possibly due to assimilation.

In the 1860s, the synagogue collapsed from lack of maintenance, and with that the Jewish identity of the community ceased to exist. During the Second World War, there were 25,000 Jewish refugees in Shanghai. Their descendants may still be keeping the Jewish faith alive in China.

PEOPLE AND
LANGUAGES

POPULATION

China has 9,596,960 square kilometres of land, more than the United States of America but less than Russia or Canada. It is divided into 28 provinces, including Taiwan, and has a population of about 1.3 billion people, compared to 290 million in the United States of America.

The majority of the population (92 per cent) is of Han (汉) ethnicity. There are 55 other ethnic minorities, the most numerous being the Zhuang (壮) (15.6 million), the Manchus (满) (8.8 million), the Miaos (苗) (7.4 million), the Uighurs (维吾尔) (7.2 million), the Yi (彝) (6.6 million), the Tujias (突厥) (5.7 million), the Mongolians (蒙) (4.8 million) and the Tibetans (藏) (4.6 million). The Zhuangs, the Miaos and the Yi live mainly in the south-western provinces. Most of the Uighurs are in the province of Xinjiang while the Tujias live mainly in the provinces of Hunan (湖南) and Hubei (湖北).

An ethnic group may be identified by its distinct language and customs and its indigenous homeland. Some of the minorities remain relatively homogeneous because of geographical isolation and religious barriers. Others are quite mixed. For instance, it is now difficult to distinguish between Manchus and Hans because of assimilation. Although the Hans form the overwhelming majority, many of them, especially those to the north, may have mixed ancestry. The first Sui emperor and the first Tang emperor were related and were said to be of Han-Turkic origin. During the time of the Three Kingdoms, the ruler of the Wu kingdom, Sun Quan (孙权), was described as having blue eyes and reddish hair.

The larger ethnic minority groups enjoy a certain degree of self-government. There are five autonomous regions where ethnic minorities can direct their own affairs. The government provides considerable educational and financial help.

WRITTEN LANGUAGE

Although the Han written language is currently used by practically all the people in China, 21 ethnic minorities, including the Manchus, the Mongolians and the Tibetans, have their own written language. Most of these are not well-developed and are unsuitable for modern use. An example is the highly pictographic Naxi language in Yunnan. However, the government appears to be helping minorities revive and improve their languages.

THE SIMPLIFIED SCRIPT

Chinese words are monosyllabic and commonly made up of components. The components often give a hint of the pronunciation and the meaning of the word. Many words consist of a large number of strokes and are cumbersome to write. Simplified writing, with the omission of some of the strokes in the more complicated words, has long been used. It was standardised and popularised by the People's Republic of China. In the Chinese-speaking world today, only Taiwan still clings to the traditional written word form. This does not present a problem, as a person brought up in the traditional word style can usually understand the simplified type. The converse, however, may not be true.

The Han written language evolved from hieroglyphic symbols that can be traced back to the Shang dynasty. During the Zhou dynasty, when the country was fragmented into a number of autonomous states, the language existed in several different forms. It was in the third century B.C. that Qin Shi Huang's prime minister, Li Si, created the standard script known as Xiao Zhuan (小篆) and eliminated all other types of script. The present written form of the Chinese language evolved from Xiao Zhuan.

SPOKEN LANGUAGES AND DIALECTS

The 56 ethnic groups in China use 201 spoken languages or dialects. The most commonly spoken language is Mandarin, which is used regularly by 867 million people. The least commonly used is the Khakas language with only ten fluent speakers in a small ethnic group in the Heilongjiang (黑龙江) province.

The term "Mandarin" is of Portuguese origin and refers to a Chinese court official. The "official language" (官话) spoken by these officials in the imperial court came to be called Mandarin. Now called *putonghua* (普通话) or "common language" within China, it is essentially the Beijing dialect spoken without the rolling of the tongue.

Pin-Yin and *Zhu-Yin* Symbols

Non-native speakers of Mandarin often pronounce Chinese words inaccurately in Mandarin. A system indicating the pronunciation of Chinese words using the Roman alphabet called *pin-yin* (拼音), or phonetic spelling, was adopted by China in 1958.

SPEAKING IN TONGUES

Chinese dialects vary greatly from one another. Many of the northern dialects are mutually intelligible to some extent, but the southern dialects can be as different from one another as English and French. For instance, a non-Cantonese would not be able to understand the Cantonese dialect unless he has learned it. Most southern dialects are thus unintelligible to northerners.

The *pin-yin* system standardises pronunciation, using symbols to indicate different intonations. The system is now widely used and its application has been extended to Romanised Chinese. The difficulty encountered in the use of Romanised Chinese is that many Chinese words have the same pronunciation and intonation even when they have different meanings. Reading Chinese in Romanised form may therefore require a certain amount of guessing.

Prior to the introduction of the *pin-yin* system, there already existed a system of phonetic symbols to indicate the pronunciation and intonation of words. Called *zhu-yin* symbols (注音符号), it is a serviceable system that is still used in Taiwan.

Peculiarities of the Chinese Language

There are four intonations used in pronouncing Chinese words. Two words can have the same pronunciation but different intonations. A person can be misunderstood if he pronounces a word correctly but uses the wrong intonation.

The Chinese grammar is completely different from English. There are no singular or plural forms of nouns. Adjectives are used to indicate the number. To the Chinese, "many man" can only mean "many men", and it is unnecessary to use a different form of the noun. There are no tenses in Chinese verbs, and adverbs are used to indicate the time element. For instance, to the Chinese, "I go yesterday" is clear enough and there is no need to alter the verb. The Chinese language has its own word order in the sentence structure. To convert a remark into a question, one simply adds the word *ma* (吗) at the end.

BETWEEN ENGLISH AND CHINESE

Two difficulties commonly encountered by the Chinese in learning English are grammar and sentence structure. The Chinese student must be familiar with English grammar and must learn to express himself in the English way without resorting to Chinese sentence structure and expressions.

TRADITIONAL
LITERATURE

POETRY

Traditional Chinese poetry and music are inseparably intertwined. Chinese poems are essentially lyrics. The number of words per line as well as the rhyming and the intonation of words are all strictly prescribed.

Shi Jing

Compiled during the Zhou dynasty, *Shi Jing* (诗经), or *The Classic of Poetry*, is the earliest collection of Chinese poems. It contains 305 poems and was part of the curriculum for Confucius' students. One-hundred-and-sixty poems in the book are folk songs (风) that were collected from 15 regions in the country. One-hundred-and-five poems are in the "aesthetic" (雅) section, of which 71 were songs for entertainment at informal dinners and 34 for official banquets. The remaining 40 poems (颂) were meant for religious ceremonies and were sung at dances. All the poems were originally sung with instrumental accompaniment but the musical notes have long been lost. The poems are well-written and concise, with the economy of words being typical of old Chinese writing.

Tang Poetry

After the end of the Zhou dynasty, Chinese poetry continued to develop over a period of more than 800 years, coming to full blossom during the Tang dynasty. According to a compilation made during the reign of Kangxi in the Qing dynasty, there existed almost 50,000 Tang poems by more than 2,200 authors.

The cream of the crop is represented in a collection of 300 Tang poems that is now widely known.

There are two categories in classical Tang poetry; one has five words per line (五言), and the other, seven (七言). Each category is further divided into two patterns. One pattern is limited to four lines per poem (绝), the other, eight (律). There are therefore four different patterns. Apart from these stipulations, there are strict rules regarding the rhyming and intonation of words. For instance, in a seven-worded line, the second, fourth and sixth words must have a certain intonation.

The styles of Chinese poems are made to suit Chinese words, which are monosyllabic. Translated into English, Chinese poems invariably lose much of their beauty. For example, Tang dynasty poet Zhang Ji (张继) wrote a poem when he was depressed after failing the imperial examination. On his way home, the riverboat he was travelling on happened to be moored by the side of the Maple Bridge for the night. Being insomniac, he wrote:

月落乌啼霜满天 江枫渔火对愁眠
姑苏城外寒山寺 夜半钟声到客船

The poem can be freely translated as follows although much of its beauty is lost:

The cackling of crows pierces the moonless night,
As frost fills the sky.
Sorrow deprives me of my sleep,
While I gaze at the fishing lamps,
By the Maple Bridge.
Far away outside Gusu City,
The tolling of the Hanshan Temple bell reaches my boat,
In the still of the night.

A translation by Sun Da Yu (孙大雨) is better but still somewhat awkward:

> *The moon is sinking; a crow croaks a-dreaming;*
> *'Neath the night sky the frost casts a haze;*
> *Few fishing-boat lights of th' riverside village*
> *Are dozing off in their mutual sad gaze.*
> *From the Cold Hill Bonzary outside*
> *The city wall of Gusu town,*
> *The resounding bell is tolling its clangour*
> *At midnight to the passenger ship down.*

Because of the need to conform to requirements governing the rhyming, intonation and number of words used in a work, Chinese poems are usually extremely terse. This severe economy of words often renders the meaning ambiguous, Zhang Ji's poem being a case in point. The two words *jiang* (江) and *feng* (枫) have been variously interpreted as "riverside maples" or "riverside village" as in the above translation. Actually, the author was referring to two bridges – the Jiang (River) Bridge and the Feng (Maple) Bridge. In fact, the title of his poem is *Night Mooring at Feng Bridge*.

Besides the rigid forms, two more liberal types of poetry were also popular during the Tang dynasty: the "old poetry" (古诗) and the "new musical house" (新乐府). These genres are narrative in nature and not restricted in length. The lines may have a variable number of words and the style is flowing and refreshing. The themes are mostly about specific events or persons and are often sad. Many are anti-establishment criticisms. For instance, famous Tang dynasty poet Bai Jüyi (白居易) wrote a long, touching poem about a grey-haired palace maid. Selected as one of the 3,000 royal concubines, she entered the palace at the age of 16. By the age of 60, she was still living in the secluded quarters and had never seen the emperor's face.

There were many excellent poets during the Tang dynasty. Li Bai (李白) and Du Fu (杜甫) were especially outstanding. Li Bai, dubbed "The God of Poetry", was what we would call a Bohemian today. He was often drunk but produced the best works with flair in the intoxicated state. He drowned while trying to catch the moon in a lake. Du Fu, dubbed "The Saint of Poetry", lived an impoverished life and moved from place to place because of war. Most of his poems are sad.

The Song *Ci* (Verse)

Towards the end of the Tang dynasty, a new type of poetry called the *ci* (词), or verse, began to develop. It entered its golden period during the Song dynasty. It is a very restrictive form of poetry. Briefly, there are at least 150 different patterns that specify the total length of a poem, the number of words in each phrase, and the required rhyming and intonation of the words. Each pattern has a colourful name. To write a *ci*, one must first decide which pattern to use. In fact, the word "write" is not used. One is said to "fill in" the *ci*. In essence, the *ci* pattern provides the blank spaces for one to fill in the words. *Ci* is arguably the highest form of Chinese poetry. A few Song scholars known for their *ci* were Su Dongpo (苏东坡), Zhou Bangyan (周邦彦), Li Yu (李煜), and Li Qingzhao (李清照).

A LEADER AND A POET

Mao Zedong once wrote a *ci* comparing himself with the great emperors in Chinese history. He concluded that he surpassed them all. Mao's *ci* became a national sensation. It is possible that every literate Chinese at the time could recite it.

YUAN SONGS AND DRAMAS

The *ci* poetry of the Tang and Song dynasties evolved into pure musical lyrics during the Yuan dynasty. Many songs were produced for entertainment in theatres and "green houses" (青楼), which are similar to Japanese *geisha* houses. The lyrics follow the general pattern of *ci* and are bound by similar rules although certain variations are allowed. A set pattern with specifications and a fixed melody attached to it is called a "tune card" (曲牌). There are several hundred different cards, each with its own name and specifications for the wording pattern of the lyrics and an accompanying tune. A song is created when one fits the wording into the set pattern. Thus, different songs based on the same tune card have the same melody and wording pattern but different lyrics.

Yuan songs gave rise to Yuan dramas. Traditional Chinese drama or opera reached its peak during the Yuan dynasty. There has been no radical change from the Yuan dramas to the Chinese operas of today. The stage is essentially bare with few props; the acting is mostly symbolic. The lifting of one leg signifies the crossing of the threshold of a door. Holding a certain stick signifies riding a horse. The heavily made-up actors in colourful costumes act and sing out the story with tunes dictated by the tune cards. The singing is interrupted now and then by plain dialogue. A Chinese orchestra with string, wind and percussion instruments supports the entire play. The stories, based on history or folk tales, are well-known to the audience. In the old days, women were excluded from acting in the drama, and men played all the female roles.

Because of the diversity of dialect groups and the vastness of the land, Chinese opera naturally came to be divided into many branches according to dialect and geographical region. In the north, Beijing opera or *jingju* (京剧) and *kunju* (昆剧) from Kunshan near Shanghai are the most refined and popular. Among the Cantonese-speaking people in the south and overseas, the Cantonese opera or *yueju* (粤剧) has many faithful fans among the older generation.

MING AND QING LONG NOVELS

While the Tang dynasty was known for its poetry, the Song dynasty for its *ci* and the Yuan dynasty for its songs and drama, the Ming and Qing dynasties were the golden age of long novels.

At the end of the Han dynasty, the country was fragmented into three kingdoms: Wei, Wu and Shu. They fought one another incessantly for a long period before they were all finally unified as one nation under the Jin dynasty. The events of the period were dramatised by Ming dynasty author Luo Guanzhong (罗贯中) in the first long Chinese novel ever written, *San Guo Yan Yi* (三国演义) or *The Popular Story of the Three Kingdoms*. He based his story on the factual *Annals of the Three Kingdoms* by Chen Shou (陈寿) of the Jin dynasty. The novel consists of 120 chapters, covering a period of 97 years (168 – 265), and describes the fascinating details of the political and military intrigues among the three kingdoms. It is a mix of fact and fiction but is so captivating and so widely read that the version of history it has generated is better known than the factual account written by the court historian. Generally considered to be the best of the classical Chinese novels, it has been translated into English under the title *Romance of the Three Kingdoms* by C.H. Brewitt-Taylor and also under the title *The Three Kingdoms* by Moss Roberts.

The next most popular novel is *Shui Hu Quan Zhuan* (水浒全传), or *Water Margin,* written by Shi Naian (施耐庵), a Ming author. The story, mostly fictional, is set in the declining years of the Northern Song dynasty, a period when corruption among government officials was widespread. It relates the tale of 108 men who fall foul of the law and take to the hills to become bandits. The men are portrayed as Chinese Robin Hoods, righteous heroes fighting against rapacious officials. At the same time, the novel seems to condone murder and even cannibalism although few of the characters described appear to have any justification in commiting their crimes, which includes the killing of innocent people. The version of the novel that is currently widely available and is likely to be the one most commonly read consists of only 70 chapters, whilst the older version has 120 chapters. It is believed that Jin Shentan (金圣叹), a Qing scholar, edited the book and deleted the last 50 chapters, which were considered to be poorly written. The story has been serialised on Chinese television. Among the English translations are *All Men are Brothers* by Pearl S. Buck and *Outlaws of the Marsh* by Sydney Shapiro. There are at least two other English translations.

While *The Three Kingdoms* and *Shui Hu Quan Zhuan* are mainly about men's affairs, which the fairer sex may not find interesting, *Hong Lou Meng* (红楼梦), or *Dream of the Red Chamber,* is mostly about women. The first 80 chapters of this romantic novel of high literary value was written by Cao Xuejin (曹雪芹) but it was not completed until 1791, almost 30 years after the author's death, when another writer named Gao E (高鹗) presented what was claimed to be the last 40 chapters of the novel, reconstructed from Cao Xuejin's notes. The story is about the rise and fall of a rich, influential family with many members. The main character is an adolescent boy who grows up in luxury among pretty girl companions and maids. He finds himself having to choose between two girls for a wife. He loves one but the family elders favour the other. The ending is tragic. The moral is Buddhist; all things in life eventually come to naught. The book has been translated into English by Yang Xiang and Gladys Yang, and also by Chi-Chen Wang.

Another popular long novel is *Jin Ping Mei* (金瓶梅), written by Wang Fengzhou (王凤洲) under the pen name Xiao Xiaosheng (笑笑生) and translated as *Golden Lotus* by Clement Egerton. The novel, 100 chapters long, is about a rich, wicked man who has at his disposal half-a-dozen concubines and several maids and mistresses. The original, unabridged version is pornographic in nature, but the "cleansed" version is a literary masterpiece.

There is an interesting side story, probably untrue, about this particular novel. It seems that the author, Wang Fengzhou, had been wronged by an official and wanted to have his revenge. The official was known for his addiction to pornographic literature and, taking advantage of this, Wang Fengzhou wrote the book, coated the pages with arsenic, and had it presented to the official. At the time, it was usual for one reading a book to wet the fingertip with saliva to turn over the thin rice pages. The official was so enthralled by the book that he could not stop reading it. He died after reading the last page.

A novel that is popular with both adults and children is *Xi You Ji* (西游记), translated as *Journey to the West* by W.J.F. Jenner. It was written by Wu Chengen (吴承恩), a Qing scholar. Based on Tang dynasty monk Xuan Zang's journey to India to bring back Buddhist scriptures, the novel is mainly fictional but highly entertaining. The monk's three disciples battled numerous demons along the way to protect their master. It seems that the monk had gone through ten previous reincarnations in celibacy. All the male demons were keen to have a piece of his flesh, which would confer immortality, and all the female demons were keen to have relations with him.

There are many other long novels written in the Ming and Qing periods of lesser fame and popularity.

CLASSICAL LITERATURE

A great deal of old Chinese classical literature, besides that related to Confucianism, has to do with historical records. There are 24 volumes of annals of dynasties written by court historians. The first volume is *The Annals* written by Sima Qian, covering the history from the ancient periods to the Han dynasty. The last volume is about Ming history.

The best-known collection of old essays is *Gu Wen Guan Zhi* (古文观止) or *The Best of Old Essays,* edited by Wu Chucai (吴楚材), a Qing scholar. It is a compilation of 222 essays selected from the Zhou through the Ming dynasties. Writings of the Yuan and Qing dynasties were conspicuously left out, reflecting the scholar's ethnic prejudices. Editors of school textbooks for the Chinese language draw heavily from material in this book.

A rather unique book on history written by a Song official named Sima Guang (司马光) with the help of several other scholars chronicles events over several dynasties that could serve as lessons in history. Entitled *Zi Zhi Tong Jian* (资治通鉴), or *Aid to Government,* it was intended to be a reference for rulers and a "mirror" for them to reflect upon. However, it is doubtful if any subsequent emperor became any wiser by reading the book.

Beginning from the Song dynasty, children starting school were taught the *San Zi Jing* (三字经), or *Three-worded Jing.* They had to learn the *Jing* by heart even before they would have able to understand it. However, compulsory learning of the *Jing* was discontinued when the new school system became popular around the end of the Qing dynasty and the beginning of the Republic of China. The *Jing* consists of 177 words arranged in 59 phrases of three words each. It embodies basic Confucianism, the chronology of the dynasties as well as a dash of geography, mathematics and biology. Besides dispensing general knowledge, the book emphasises the importance of teaching and learning, as evidenced in the following excerpts:

Men are born good	人之初
And similar in nature.	性本善
They become different	性相近
By influence of nurture.	习相远
Man's nature goes wayward	苟不教
With neglect of teaching.	性乃迁
Full attention is needed	教之道
For proper upbringing.	贵以专
Jade that is not carved	玉不琢
Does not rate as jewellery.	不成器
Man who is unlearned	人不学
Is ignorant of morality.	不知义

Some folk verses from the past, collections of sayings reflecting conventional wisdom, are still frequently quoted in writing and conversation. Examples include:

Long distance brings out the horse's stamina.	路遥知马力
Long association reveals a man's true colours.	日久见人心
Draw a tiger; you draw the skin and not the bones.	画虎画皮难画骨
Know a man; you know the face and not the heart.	知人知面不知心
Men die for wealth.	人为财死
Birds die for food.	鸟为食亡

NEWER LITERATURE

A new form of Chinese poetry was introduced by Hu Shih in 1917, much to the annoyance of traditionalists. It is free in style, there being no restrictions on length, number of words or intonation. Rhyming is optional. Acceptance came slowly. A notable follower, nevertheless, was the writer Guo Moruo (郭沫若), who, surprisingly, was an accomplished traditional poet.

Hu Shih was also the foremost advocate for the use of vernacular Chinese in place of the classical *wen yan* (文言), an old Chinese language text form characterised by terseness, a severe economy of words and the usage of certain outdated words. This movement occurred during the height of the May Fourth Movement of 1919 when young, patriotic Chinese intellectuals clamoured for reform as a means of national salvation.

It was around this time that there emerged many outstanding writers who wrote on the shortcomings of Chinese society and the Chinese people. One of the best-known writers of the era was Lu Xun (鲁迅), whose satirical stories were extremely piercing. One of his short novels, *Kuang Ren Ri Ji (*狂人日记*)*, or *The Diary of a Madman,* highlighted the ills of Chinese society. Another story, a bestseller entitled *A Q Zheng Zhuan* (阿Q正转), or *The Biography of A-Q,* has as its protagonist A-Q, a character who personifies the pathetic characteristics of the Chinese. This particular work has probably been read by every student of Chinese literature.

In the next few decades, the literary stage in China was crowded with such young and talented writers as Ba Jin (巴金), Mao Dun (矛盾), Cao Yu (曹禺) and Tian Han (田汉). Most of the works sought to expose unhealthy traditional family structures and injustice in society due to predatory landlords, warlords and foreign interests. In later years, many left-leaning writers blamed China's ills on the Nationalist (Kuomintang) government and heaped praises on the Communists.

Lin Yutang (林语堂), editor of a magazine in 1930s, came from a preacher's family and had spent some years attending postgraduate school at Harvard. He was known for his "humour literature" and was credited with translating the word "humour" into Chinese, there being no exact equivalent of the word in Chinese. Pearl S. Buck meanwhile was an American writer who had spent long years in China. She wrote the novel *The Good Earth* and attained worldwide fame, later winning the Nobel Prize in literature. She met Lin Yutang in Shanghai in 1933 and encouraged him to write a book in English on Chinese culture for Westerners. Lin published his book *My Country and My People* in English in 1935. It became a bestseller in the United States of America. Two years later, he published his second book in English, entitled *The Importance of Living*, which was widely acclaimed. Lin was probably the first Chinese to publish a book in English. He headed Nanyang University in Singapore for a brief period in the 1950s.

The image of the Chinese writer as a poor, struggling craftsman changed in the 1950s and the 1960s when at least two writers became very rich from writing. One of them was Jin Yong (金庸) who wrote 15 long novels on martial arts, similar in theme and style to the movie *Crouching Tiger, Hidden Dragon*. The other author was a lady named Qiong Yao (琼瑶) who wrote 52 long stories and a large number of short stories, all about love and romance.

In 1992, Bo Yang (柏杨) of Taiwan published his controversial book *The Ugly Chinaman,* describing the undesirable and despicable aspects of Chinese traditional behaviour. He drove home the point that a long-established civilisation would not necessarily have graciousness in culture unless accompanied by self-renewal. Another well-respected contemporary writer is Yu Qiuyu (余秋雨), known for his books on travel, focusing on history, culture and civilisation.

THE CONTROVERSIAL NOBEL LAUREATE

In 2000, the Nobel Prize in Literature was awarded for the first time to a Chinese. The laureate was Gao Xingjian (高行健). His best-known book, *Soul Mountain* (灵山), was published in 1999. Gao resides in France and is *persona non grata* in China because of his 1993 publication of the play *Fugitives,* written against the background of the Tiananmen Square incident. The award incurred general controversy and China's displeasure (China had earlier nominated Ba Jin for the prize). *Soul Mountain* is a book on Gao's journey through Sichuan in 1983. The book is unique in style; it has no clear plot or storyline and is by all accounts difficult for the general public to understand.

INTERESTING
PROVERBS

RIDING THE TIGER (骑虎难下)

This saying is familiar to many Westerners, but its meaning is often not fully understood. It is usually taken to mean a dangerous situation, but its actual meaning is deeper. The meaning implicit in the saying is that there is no future in carrying on, yet one has no other choice. He who dismounts a tiger gets eaten. The proverb originated during the South-North dynasty. A reluctant general was made to lead a rebellion, which apparently was doomed to failure. Sensing the hopeless situation, he wanted to give up his position and leave but was told that there was no way for him to "get off the tiger" safely.

THE FRONTIERSMAN LOST A HORSE (塞翁失马)

The English equivalent of this saying is "A blessing in disguise". It has its origins in a tale told in the Han dynasty. An old frontiersman lost a horse and was being consoled by his neighbours when he remarked that what had occurred was not necessarily bad luck. A few months later, his horse returned with another horse. The neighbours offered the frontiersman their congratulations, but the old man thought that the turn of events need not necessarily be good fortune. A little while later, his son took the new horse out for a ride but fell off and broke a leg. To the neighbours who expressed their sympathy, the frontiersman said that it might not have been a bad thing. A few months later, a war broke out and all able-bodied young men were conscripted into the army. Most were not expected to return alive. However, the frontiersman's son was exempted from military duty because he had a limp, once again proving that the old man's words were right.

IN THE MELON PATCH AND UNDER THE PLUM TREE (瓜田李下)

The proverb means one should avoid a situation that may cause suspicion. Literally, it advises that one should not bend down to put on shoes in a melon patch, or raise one's arms to adjust a hat under a plum tree, lest one be suspected of stealing melons and plums. The saying came from an ancient verse that was quoted by a Tang official when he advised the emperor to avoid awkward situations.

PASSING FOR A *YU* PLAYER (滥竽充数)

This saying applies to a charlatan who tries to pass himself off as being competent or skilful in a certain area of knowledge or practice. During the Warring States period, the king of the Qi state loved music played on the *yu*, a wind instrument. He kept 300 *yu* players in his employ, including one who could not play the instrument at all. However, the fraud managed to escape detection because the musicians usually played as a group and he could bluff his way through the performances. This *yu* player, who was not really a *yu* player, enjoyed all the rewards of his position until a new king ascended to the throne and asked the musicians to take turns playing solo. The pretender hastily ran away.

TRIMMING THE FEET TO FIT THE SHOES (削足就履)

This phrase refers to an extremely unwise and irrational method used to solve a problem. The saying came from the Spring-Autumn period when the king of the Jin state had his own son killed in order to resolve a family dispute.

THREE MEN MAKE A TIGER COME TRUE (三人成虎)

This particular phrase implies that a rumour becomes convincing if oft repeated. Dating from the Warring States period, the proverb was coined when a high official in the Wei state was assigned to a posting far away from the capital. In those days, officials in the outlying areas were often summoned back to the capital and executed by the king whenever he heard rumours about their disloyalty or attempts to foment rebellion. Hoping to protect himself from malicious hearsay, the official asked the king whether he would believe that there was a tiger on the main street of the capital if someone reported sighting one. The king replied that he would not. The official then asked the king whether he would believe it if a second man also claimed to have sighted the tiger. The king hesitated a moment and said that he might begin to wonder if there really were a tiger roaming the main street. Finally, the official asked the king whether he would be convinced the story of the tiger were real if the sighting was confirmed by a third man. The king admitted that if three men had reported so, he probably would believe that there indeed was a tiger on the main street. Having made his point, the official said that he could easily become a victim of false rumour if he were posted far away. The king, having gained an understanding of the official's concern, promised never to doubt him.

NO SILVER IS BURIED HERE (此地无银三百两)

This phrase is about foolish people who deceive themselves. The saying comes from a folk tale about a foolish man who had accumulated a fortune amounting to 300 taels of silver. For safekeeping, he buried the silver in the ground. Concerned that someone might find out where he hid his treasure and steal it, he erected a sign over the site that said, "300 taels of silver are not buried here". His equally foolish neighbour stole the silver and to cover up the theft added a sign that said, "The neighbour next door did not steal the silver".

BETWEEN 50 PACES AND 100 PACES (五十步笑百步)

The English equivalent of this saying is "pot calling the kettle black". Mencius introduced the proverb in his dialogue with the king of the Liang state. The Liang king was aggressive and often committed his state to war, leading to the deaths of a number of his subjects. However, he took pride in the fact that his people were well-fed, and he criticised neighbouring states for neglecting their people's welfare. Mencius told him that a soldier who ran back 50 paces in a battle had no reason to ridicule another soldier who retreated 100 paces. The Liang king was no more benevolent than the other kings, Mencius insisted.

THE DREAM ENDED BEFORE THE MILLET WAS COOKED (黄粱一梦)

The English equivalent of this phrase is "Life is but a dream". A parable written in the Tang dynasty tells of a poverty-stricken young scholar who fails the imperial examination and meets a Daoist monk at an inn. He laments his miserable fortune. The monk hands him a porcelain pillow and tells him to sleep on it to get his wish. While the innkeeper gets ready to cook a millet meal, the scholar falls asleep and dreams of passing the imperial examination with flying colours. He is appointed as an official and marries a beautiful girl. They have many children. The scholar is then promoted successively until he becomes the prime minister. He leads the army to victory against invaders and, at the height of his career, has everything he has ever wanted. His lives a good life for several decades, passing away at the age of 80. At this point, the young scholar wakes up from his dream to find that the millet meal has still not been cooked. The young man then realises that all the wealth and fame on Earth is short-lived.

DRAINING THE POND DRY FOR THE FISH (涸泽求渔)

This saying conveys the message that a highly effective method used to accomplish a task may leave nothing for the future. A somewhat similar saying in English would be "To kill the goose that lays the golden eggs". During the Warring State period, the militarily weak Jin state was invaded. The king held a conference with his ministers to discuss the defence of the state. A strategy presented to the king was likened to "draining the pond dry for the fish"; it would be very effective but could not be repeated if the state were invaded again.

ARTS AND CRAFTS

CALLIGRAPHY AND PAINTING

The Chinese art of calligraphy and painting is unique. It owes its development to the invention of the Chinese brush, ink and paper more than 2,000 years ago.

Archaeological finds have indicated that early Chinese painting began with the decoration of ceramic wares 7,000 years ago in the New Stone Age. The Chinese brush was probably invented in the third century B.C., when the art of papermaking was in development. Chinese ink, invented in the same period, is made of lampblack and glue, produced in the form of hardened ink cakes or sticks. The preferred lampblack or soot comes from burnt pine or *tung* oil, and the glue is usually made from animal horns or hides. When the ink cake is ground on a stone slab and mixed with water, black ink is produced and mixed to the desired density by a painter. Chinese ink has the property of not fading easily even after centuries of display.

Chinese brush writing had the dual role of communication and art. With the inventions of the Western ink pen, the ballpoint pen and the computer, it is now seldom used in producing documents. Even students in China no longer have to practise brush writing. Chinese brush calligraphy, nevertheless, has remained a form of art, greatly appreciated by those immersed in Chinese culture.

There are five common styles of calligraphy: *zhuan* (篆), *li* (隶), *kai* (楷), *cao* (草) and *xing* (行). *Zhuan* is an ancient script no longer used except as an art form. *Li* is a rather handsome script and again is used mainly for its artistic style. *Kai* is the current gold standard of writing and its variations are used in printing. *Cao* is generally translated as "cursive" but should be more appropriately termed "irregular". It is the most artistic of all the scripts, but the style is so individualistic that it is often difficult to decipher. *Xing* script is a blend of *kai* and *cao* and is the usual form of handwriting. If one's handwriting leans too much towards the *cao* style, it simply cannot be made out with ease and is comparable to the proverbial doctor's handwriting.

Chinese painting has a long and complicated history that is difficult to summarise. Early Chinese paintings in the Shang and Zhou dynasties were mainly animal and human forms painted on pottery and bronze wares. By the first century, when Buddhism had spread to China and was beginning to flourish, many painters started to turn to religious themes. There was a mushrooming of mural paintings depicting Buddhist deities in temples and grottoes from the South-North dynasty through to the Song dynasty. Simultaneously, paintings of landscapes, animals and plants began to develop. These attained great popularity in the Tang and Song periods. Two separate styles of landscape painting emerged. One school of painters used only black ink but cleverly varied the density of the ink to produce different shades. The other school resorted to the use of mineral pigments to produce colourful pictures. A "flower-and-bird" school branched out and developed a style characterised by a great economy of line.

After the Song dynasty, Chinese painting underwent marked changes in style. Different schools, each with its regional flavour, made their appearance and tended to influence one another. Their general framework, nevertheless, remained Chinese. The recent crop of artists such as Qi Baishi (齐白石), Huang Binhong (黄宾鸿), Wu Changshuo (吴昌硕), Ren Bonian (任伯年), Pan Tianshou (潘天寿) and Fu Baoshi (傅抱石) have modified the traditional style with their own creativity to produce distinctive works. In the past century, the relatively impressionistic Chinese painting has been strongly influenced by the meticulous realism of Western painting. The style initially originated from Western missionaries but was later adopted by China's own artists like Xu Beihong (徐悲鸿), Lin Fengmian (林凤眠), Liu Haisu (刘海粟), and Wu Guanzhong (吴冠中), who had studied oil painting in France. They injected Western influences into the composition and the brushwork of their paintings to create refreshing new styles. However, some traditionalists are not happy with this break from the old styles.

A MODERN CHINESE PAINTER

Zhang Daqian (張大千) was perhaps the most remarkable recent Chinese painter. He was extremely versatile, being adept in a wide range of styles from the conventional to the abstract. He was especially known for his talent in copying works of old masters. His "fakes" could get past the most discerning experts. His enthusiasm in the old styles moved him to spend more than two years in Dunhuang (敦煌) copying the murals of the South-North, Sui and Tang periods in the Mogao (莫高) grottoes. He travelled widely in Europe and America, and his exposure to Western contemporary art led him to create a unique splashed-ink and splashed-colour style.

Although Chinese paintings generally lean towards the free-flowing, spontaneous and expressive style known as *xieyi* (写意), they usually do not enter the realm of abstract representation. A more deliberate and scrupulous style, called *gongbi* (工笔), uses extremely fine, meticulous brushstrokes to produce detailed pictures. Some painters try for the best of two worlds by blending the *xieyi* and *gongbi* styles.

Traditional Chinese painters place overwhelming emphasis on the mastery of the brushstroke. Each stroke of the brush is definitive; it cannot be revoked or redone. The student usually acquires the brushstroke technique as a prerequisite to painting. Hence, calligraphy is an inseparable part of painting. The painter usually studies the intended scene or object at length so as to gain an in-depth perception of its aesthetic effects. He then develops the brushwork to bring out his impression. Once the painter is happy with his painting of a particular scene or object, he can readily produce several paintings of the same theme with limited variations with his well-practised brushstrokes within a short period of time. Therein lies a fault of Chinese painting. A certain degree of staleness inevitably creeps in when the artist produces a large number of paintings of the same theme, as often occurs.

Nevertheless, since the founding of the Peoples' Republic of China, Chinese painters have ventured into a wide range of artistic experimentation, freely combining traditional forms with Western techniques. They have delved deeply into the realities of life for new themes and are not confined to the old restrictive subject matters.

A MATTER OF PERCEPTION

A unique characteristic of Chinese landscape painting is that perspective is often ignored; distant and near objects can appear to be of the same size. The explanation is that the purpose of landscape painting should be to depict the objects of nature as they are and not simply to reflect the surface features of the scene.

Traditional Chinese painting depends on the use of the Chinese brush and paper. Brushes have pointed tips and are made of goat, wolf or badger hair. They are of different sizes so as to facilitate the painting of fine and bold strokes. The Chinese invented paper in the Western Han dynasty, but the use of a special type of absorbent paper, known as *xuan* (宣), did not come about until the Yuan dynasty. Prior to the invention of paper, painting was done on fabric and silk.

THE IMAGE AND THE WORD

Poetry is closely linked to traditional Chinese painting. A few lines of poetry, whether quoted or composed by the artist, are often inscribed on a painting. There is a "Three-in-One Art Society" in Singapore founded by the late Wu Tsai Yen (吳在炎), who painted with his finger instead of a brush. The name emphasises that painting, calligraphy and poetry are inseparable and that the complete painter should be proficient in all three.

CERAMICS

In ceramics or pottery, a mass of pliable earth is mixed with water and moulded to a desired shape and then hardened by high heat. The term "porcelain" usually refers to a ware made of clay containing kaolin. It is covered with a glaze and fired at a temperature of at least 1,200 degrees Celsius. It is resonant when tapped. Porcelain is called *ci* (瓷) in Chinese. The term *tao* (陶) refers to less-refined ceramics.

Chinese pottery has a history of 7,000 years, going back to the Neolithic period. More than 3,000 years ago, the Shang people were able to produce wares fired to 1,000 degrees Celsius. Coarse "proto-porcelain" ceramics with lead glaze appeared in the Warring States period. Real porcelain wares in the form of celadon porcelain and black porcelain were first produced in the Han dynasty. The Tang dynasty saw further improvements in pottery techniques with the production of the famous Tang tri-colour figurines. Many of the Han and Tang pottery wares, human and animal figurines, and miniature buildings were burial objects discovered in tombs.

A great leap in the ceramic industry occurred in the Song dynasty when many famous kilns were set up, each with its own specialty. This rapid development continued into the Yuan dynasty. The technique of producing underglaze (with coloured painting under transparent glaze) reached maturity. The production of blue-and-white and red underglaze wares attained a high standard. The kiln at Jingdezhen (景德镇) came to be known for its advanced techniques and production of large wares. The subsequent Ming dynasty took the production of blue-and-white wares to new heights. Qing dynasty potters came up with the world-renowned five-coloured wares. After that period, the Chinese ceramic industry declined as political turmoil took its toll on the production of Chinese crafts.

INVENTIONS AND
MEDICINE

INVENTIONS

China led the world in technological advances until the Qing dynasty. Its people were inventive and innovative. Unfortunately, while many of China's past inventions were undoubtedly incredible in their time, the Chinese, as a rule, failed to go the distance. They stopped at the inventions without working out the underlying principles or striving for much further improvement. As a result, they missed the train of scientific conceptual theory that carried the West into the modern age.

Nonetheless, four old Chinese inventions are of noteworthy significance: the compass, paper, printing and gunpowder. The first compass appeared some 2,500 years ago. Over time, refinements and improvements to its design made the compass an indispensable tool in navigation and sailing. Paper was invented by Cai Lun (蔡伦) in the first century, during the Han dynasty. Printing was invented about seven hundred years later, in the early eighth century, during the Tang dynasty. It was also during the Tang dynasty that the Daoist sect apparently stumbled onto the invention of explosives. Many self-proclaimed Daoist masters, engaged in alchemy and the making of longevity and immortality drugs, would mix various substances in a pot and apply high heat to it for days. This led to the accidental discovery that the application of heat to a mixture of sulphur, nitre (potassium nitrate) and carbon would cause an explosion. Using this knowledge, the Chinese developed explosives that could be used in warfare, albeit in a crude manner. Ironically, the civilisation that discovered what would eventually evolve into gunpowder would be introduced to a more effective use for it only when Western nations brought their soldiers and gunboats to China at end of the nineteenth century.

The Chinese also invented the first device to detect seismic activities, or earthquakes, based on the reverse pendulum principle, although they never improved upon it. Other Chinese inventions include the ship rudder, the canal lock, stirrups, the crossbow, the iron plough, the wheelbarrow, the hot air balloon, a toy helicopter rotor, the kite, and the folding umbrella.

The ancient Chinese took a strong interest in astronomy as well and it formed the basis for their practice of divination. It appears that the Chinese first made records of solar and lunar eclipses and meteor showers some 3,000 years ago. By the Han dynasty, they were able to make fairly accurate predictions of eclipses.

This knowledge of astronomy was integral to the development of the Chinese calendar. Evidence suggests that the Chinese had begun using a calendar as long ago as the Shang dynasty. Through the centuries, however, the Chinese calendar has undergone frequent changes. The traditional Chinese calendar in use today is based on the movements of both the moon and the earth within the solar system. It is referred to for agricultural activities and the dates of traditional festivals.

The creation of the Chinese calendar also required a strong foundation in mathematics, which, perhaps not surprisingly, was well-developed in ancient China. The first book in China to focus purely on mathematics was compiled in the Han dynasty. It described methods to calculate area, volume, fractions and ratios. It was also during the Han dynasty that the mathematician Zu Chongzhi (祖冲之) worked out the value of pi (π) to be between 3.1415926 and 3.1415927. More than a thousand years would have to pass before a German mathematician was able to arrive at a similar figure.

Despite its numerous early inventions and advances, China lapsed into a technological backwater at the dawn of the modern age. While the nation was basking in the glory of its past civilisation, secure in the belief that it had reached the zenith above all others, the West with its scientific developments and industrial revolution simply passed it by. China found itself a backward country in the jaws of the technologically superior nations it used to consider barbarians. So it came to pass that China woke up from a sweet dream only to face a nightmare.

A NARROW POINT OF VIEW

Stagnation of scientific and technological developments in China slowly set in after the introduction of the civil service examination system in the Sui-Tang period. The examination syllabus was confined to traditional classics, so most of the young talents in China simply shunned other studies. The stifling Confucian teachings also tended to discourage the development of new concepts.

MEDICINE

The practice of pure traditional Chinese medicine largely evolved from a few old books. Among the better-known and more influential are *The Yellow Emperor's Internal Medicine* (黄帝内经), *The Treatise on Febrile Diseases* (伤寒杂病论), and *The Pharmacopoeia* (本草纲目), also known as *The Indices of Drugs*. In spite of new knowledge being accrued and new books being written, the practice of traditional Chinese medicine may be considered basically flawed because it has not evolved along the scientific path.

The Yellow Emperor's Internal Medicine

The book that laid the foundation for traditional Chinese medicine is called *The Yellow Emperor's Internal Medicine*. It is supposed to record a discussion between the Yellow Emperor and his ministers about medicine. However, the Yellow Emperor, who would have lived almost 5,000 years ago, is unlikely to have had anything to do with the book as it had probably been compiled at a later date, during the early dynasties. The final compilation and edition of the book probably took place in the Western Han period some 2,000 years ago.

The practice of medicine and its underlying concepts as described in *The Yellow Emperor's Internal Medicine* probably would not withstand modern scientific scrutiny. For instance, discussions on the development of diseases with respect to causes are shrouded in cryptic terms. Diseases are said to arise due to the interplay between *yin* and *yang* and the five natural elements: metal, wood, water, fire and earth. Under the same schema, bodily organs are classified without any apparent rationale as being under the *yin* or *yang* aspect of an element. Further, the anatomy and physiology of various organs in the human body is described inaccurately. In view of this, modern readers should consider the book to be of historical interest only.

NEEDLING PAIN

Acupuncture is described in *The Yellow Emperor's Internal Medicine* and other ancient books. This treatment may temporarily relieve pain in some situations, either through the stimulation of the release of pain-relieving endorphins or through hypnotic suggestion, but it is now known that acupuncture has no curative effect and does not affect the underlying disease in any way. At best, it may relieve pain for a short period of time.

The Treatise on Febrile Diseases

Another influential book on traditional Chinese medicine is *The Treatise on Febrile Diseases*, written by Zhang Zhongjing (张仲景), a medical practitioner in the Eastern Han dynasty about 1,800 years ago.

The book deals with the symptoms and the treatments of diseases such as infections that are associated with fever. Unfortunately, the germ theory of infection, which holds that infections were caused by micro-organisms such as bacteria and viruses, was alien to the Chinese. For instance, flu was thought to be due to the entry of "ill wind" into the body. Furthermore, as there were no reliable means of diagnosis, different types of infections could not be distinguished with certainty. Hence, although the book that has been revered and studied by Chinese medical practitioners for centuries, it is of little value based on what we know today.

The Pharmacopoeia

During the Ming dynasty, Li Shizhen (李时珍), descended from a family of medical practitioners, painstakingly compiled and classified 1,892 substances used for medicinal purposes. The resulting work, *The Pharmacopoeia*, complete with illustrations and prescriptions, is an encyclopaedia of Chinese medicine.

Medicinal substances are classified within the book under three categories, namely, inorganic matter (minerals), herbal plants and animals (insects and animal parts), all of which are known to the Chinese generically as "herbs". It should be noted that the information presented in the book on these substances was not gleaned from scientific studies but from superficial observations and anecdotal accounts. Since a typical prescription usually includes at least half-a-dozen herbs, each of which may contain a large number of properties, the useful active constituents, if present, are buried in their midst and not identified.

FROM FOLK TREATMENT TO SCIENTIFIC CURE

Li Shizhen's *Pharmacopoeia* undoubtedly contains some valid and useful information, but to go through 1,892 crude substances to extract and analyse clinically useful constituents is quite another matter, even with modern laboratory facilities. Nevertheless, this laborious task is necessary if Chinese medicine is to renew itself and contribute to modern medicine. Otherwise, one would be employing remedies with unknown properties to treat diseases that are inaccurately diagnosed.

The Future Course of Chinese Medicine

Between the declining years of the Qing dynasty and the beginning of the Republic of China, Chinese intelligentsia began to realise that China had fallen hopelessly behind the West in science and technology. They concluded that it would be futile to try to develop what they had in order to catch up with the West. Being a pragmatic people, the Chinese essentially gave up what they had developed over the course of more than 5,000 years and copied wholesale Western scientific and technological advances. They retained their culture, language and literature, but ardently assimilated what the West had to offer in such fields as the physical and biological sciences, engineering and architecture.

Medicine was no exception. Practitioners of Western medicine were trained. The Peking Union Medical College in Beijing, founded in 1906 and re-organised with the support of the Rockefeller Foundation in 1917, could match European and American medical schools in standard. However, traditional Chinese medicine continued to be practised because Western-trained doctors could not be produced fast enough. The trend in China leaned towards replacing traditional Chinese medicine with Western medicine. Unfortunately, civil war and the Japanese invasion disrupted this development.

Communist rule in China saw the resurgence of traditional Chinese medicine. After years of war, it was impossible to provide Western-type medical care to most of the people. "Barefoot doctors", trained for only two years, were sent to villages. Acupuncture, a treatment with low financial costs, was promoted. "Combined" Chinese and Western medical treatment thus became the fashion.

Initially an economic and political necessity, the promotion of traditional Chinese medicine soon took on new significance. China began to generate revenue when it attracted overseas Chinese to go to China to seek treatment. It began to export raw herbs and manufactured herbal drugs.

Practitioners of traditional Chinese medicine have come to realise that the pure traditional form of practice is out of step with the modern world. Thus, they have adopted the strategy of riding piggyback on Western medicine by claiming that Chinese medicine is "holistic" and that it enables the patient to respond better to Western treatment. Unfortunately, there appears to be no objective evidence to support the claim. There is also little or no explanation as to how Chinese medicine can be "holistic" or how it can enhance the efficacy of Western medicine.

Chinese drugs are increasingly taking on a new image through packaging. Herbs are now dispensed in manufactured tablets instead of their traditional raw forms. Patients who take high doses of these tablets over an extended period may be unaware of the potential danger of accumulated toxicity and long-term adverse effects if stringent pre-marketing testing and clinical trials were not carried out. Traditionally, herbs were boiled in water to a concentration of 70–80 per cent and consumed as a single dose, about once a day. In such cases, the toxins that are bound to be present in varying amounts in some of the herbs could presumably be adequately detoxified by the liver or excreted by the kidneys. In tablet form however, the properties of the herbs, as well as the toxins, are likely to be more concentrated. If the tablets were consumed several times a day over a relatively long period, the toxins could accumulate and overwhelm the body's detoxifying mechanisms. Furthermore, there may be side effects that lie dormant to surface only much later.

A great deal of work has been done in China to identify and extract the useful constituents in herbs and test them clinically. This is the scientific approach long practised by the West. However, success as a rule does not come easily. In 1965, Chinese researchers isolated a compound called artemisinin from a herb. Two decades passed before it was hailed by the world as an effective anti-malarial agent.

The study of herbs in itself may be insufficient in the drive to modernise traditional Chinese medicine. In fact, a clear distinction should be made between two aspects of Chinese medicine. One concerns herbs. There is no disagreement that clinically useful constituents are waiting to be discovered, extracted and tested in the multitude of Chinese medicinal herbs. This is where research on Chinese medicine, using Western scientific methods, should be concentrated. The other aspect of Chinese medicine concerns the system of practice that encompasses concepts of how diseases develop and how they can be diagnosed and treated rationally. In this area, traditional Chinese medicine is ineffectual, being out of the scientific mainstream. The valid practice of modern medicine requires knowledge of basic biological sciences and an understanding of the nature and development of diseases, and it needs the support of scientific diagnostic tests and the various modalities of treatment. All these are sadly lacking in traditional Chinese medicine.

Thus, attempts to upgrade the practice of traditional Chinese medicine to an acceptable level would amount to developing Western medicine all over again from its primitive stage. Thus, it seems that if Chinese medicine were to be developed and improved to its logical end, it would become indistinguishable from Western medicine.

THE PERSISTENCE OF TRADITIONAL CHINESE MEDICINE

The past attitude of the Chinese in assimilating Western advances suddenly appears to be lost when it comes to traditional medicine. One important ground for not discarding traditional Chinese medicine seems to be that it is inexpensive. It requires no expensive tests and equipment and no complicated treatment procedures. It seems to be a good way to contain health care costs within the affordable range but is in actual fact a false economy as ineffective treatment would add to the cost and delay the cure. Another factor is that a policy of promoting traditional Chinese medicine would appeal to ethnic Chinese and is politically expedient. However, the strongest driving force behind promoting Chinese medicine undoubtedly comes from commercial interests. There are enormous monetary implications in the trade of Chinese herbs and drugs, and the practice of traditional Chinese medicine.

THE CHINESE
CALENDAR AND
TRADITIONAL
FESTIVALS

THE CHINESE CALENDAR

The Chinese calendar is a two-tier system incorporating the features of both the lunar and solar calendars. The dates of traditional festivals are based on the lunar aspect while seasons are defined according to the earth's orbit around the sun.

In the solar calendar now used worldwide, a year is equivalent to 365 days, the amount of time it takes the earth to make one revolution around the sun. However, the actual time it takes the earth to orbit the sun is slightly longer, 365.2422 days to be exact. Hence, it is necessary to have an extra day every four years to make up the difference. The year in which this occurs, known as a leap year, is usually a number divisible by four. This, however, would amount to one day too many every 128 years, about three additional days every 400 years. This problem is resolved by omitting the "leap" in every year that is a multiple of 100 but is not divisible by 400. For instance, years 2000 and 2400, both multiples of 100, are leap years as they are divisible by 400. The years 2100 and 2200, also multiples of 100, are not leap years because they are not divisible by 400.

The lunar calendar has 12 months a year, a month being the time it takes the moon to revolve once around the earth, or the interval between a new moon and the next new moon or between a full moon and the next full moon. This time interval is between 29 and 30 days. The exact figure is 29 days,

12 hours, 44 minutes and 3 seconds. Thus, in the lunar calendar, every odd month has 30 days and every even month has 29 days. However, this would mean that there would only be 354 days a year with a remainder of 8 hours, 48 minutes and 34 seconds. Therefore, the lunar calendar has 11 leap years every 30 years to accommodate the extra time. In spite of this, compared to the solar year, the average lunar year is still about 11 days short. The shortage amounts to more than six months in 17 years. Because of this shortage, societies who follow the lunar calendar, such as people of the Islamic faith, find that their festival days do not always occur in the same season every year. For instance, the main festival equivalent to the New Year for Muslims can be in winter, spring, summer or autumn.

COUNTING THE HOURS

A remarkable coincidence exists in the way a day is divided in ancient China and the way a day is divided in the West. Traditionally, the Chinese divide the day into 12 equal units called *di-zhi* (地支), each *di-zhi* being exactly two hours in the Western measure of time. It is interesting that both the ancient Chinese and the Westerners have divided the amount of time in a day by a base of 12.

The Chinese calendar, now called the agricultural calendar (农历), was originally called the Xia calendar (夏历) because it supposedly originated in the Xia dynasty about 4,000 years ago. It has 12 unequal months a year like the solar and the lunar calendars. The first of the month is when the moon is between the sun and the earth and is totally dark. Based on this, out of 100 months, 53 have 30 days a month and 47 have 29 days a month. Again, this works out at slightly more than 354 days, about 11 days short of a year in the solar calendar. To recoup the extra days, an extra month a year is added to seven out of every 19 years. This method narrows the difference between the solar year and the Chinese calendar year to about two hours in 19 years.

Seasons are important to the Chinese, who are an agricultural society. Seasons depend on the earth's orbit around the sun rather than on the movements of the moon. Therefore, the Chinese calendar has to have input from the solar calendar with respect to seasons.

The Chinese have divided the year into 24 "climatic periods" (节气) since the time of the Warring States. These periods indicate the timing of the seasons and climatic changes, and the farmers follow them for their agricultural activities. There are six periods in each season. Thus, in the 360-degree orbit of the earth around the sun, each period lasts the amount of time it takes the earth to move 15 degrees.

The seasons are fixed according to four reference points, which are the two equinoxes and the two solstices. The solstices and equinoxes occur approximately in the middle of each season, allowing for the beginning and the end of the four seasons to be determined. The sun is directly over the earth's equator on the spring equinox, also known as the vernal equinox, around March 21, at zero degree of the earth's orbit. The sun is again directly over the equator on the autumnal equinox around September 23, when the earth is 180 degrees into its orbit. The sun is furthest from the equator, over the Tropic of Cancer, on the summer solstice around June 21 when the earth is 90 degrees into its orbit. This circumstance is repeated on the winter solstice around December 22 when the earth is 270 degrees into its orbit and the sun is over the Tropic of Capricorn.

TRADITIONAL FESTIVALS

The Chinese New Year

The Chinese New Year is the first day of the first lunar month in the Chinese calendar and generally falls near the first day of spring. The Chinese government has long ago adopted the first day of the solar year as the New Year and renamed the traditional Chinese New Year the Spring Festival. However, old traditions are not easily forgotten and most Chinese still celebrate the Chinese New Year.

A family reunion dinner is usually held on Chinese New Year's Eve. All members of a family would try to attend the dinner. On Chinese New Year's Day, people usually wear new clothes. Children wish their parents good fortune and receive red packets containing money. In fact, any unmarried family member is entitled to receive a red packet from every married member. Firecrackers are set off unless they are specifically banned. Traditionally, the celebration would go on until the fifteenth day with a programme of things to do for every day. Nowadays, most people still do not work for the first three days of the Chinese New Year. It is customary to visit relatives and friends during the season.

On the ninth day of the New Year, a traditional offering is made to the Jade Emperor in heaven. This day is supposed to mark the deity's birthday, a belief that is related to the Dao religion.

A mythical tale is associated with the Chinese New Year. In ancient times, a beast called *Nian* or "year" would emerge from the sea on Chinese New Year's Eve to eat people and destroy property. Hence, people used to keep themselves awake through Chinese New Year's Eve. Firecrackers were meant to frighten the beast away. On Chinese New Year's Day, people would congratulate each other on their safe passage through the "year" or *Nian* hazard.

Yuan Xiao (元宵) is the fifteenth day of the Chinese New Year. In ancient China, this was the night when the emperor would come out of the palace to celebrate the season with the populace. Buildings were decorated with lanterns and shows were put up on streets. The festival is no longer celebrated but traditional families would still have a sumptuous family dinner on this night to mark the end of the Chinese New Year season.

The custom of putting up new "couplets" on either side of the door for the Chinese New Year is still practised in some Chinese villages. It began in the Zhou dynasty some 2,500 years ago. Originally, a board made of peach wood with the name of a god written on it was hung on each side of the door. It was meant to chase away evil spirits. By the Ming dynasty, the practice was superseded by the display of auspicious "couplets", which are two matching lines of script written on red paper. The two lines are equal in the number of words and must match word for word. If a word on the right is a noun, the corresponding word on the left must also be one. Similarly, an adjective is matched by an adjective and a verb by a verb. The closer the match, the better the couplet. For instance, a quantitative adjective is matched by another quantitative adjective. If the adjective refers to a colour, the corresponding word on the other side is also the name of a colour. Repetitions are regarded poor in standard.

THE CHINESE ACCOUNT OF A PERSON'S AGE

According to Chinese custom, a baby is one year old at birth, as the length of a pregnancy is counted as one year. Everyone gains one year in age on New Year's Day. Thus, a baby born on Chinese New Year's Eve would be two years old on Chinese New Year's Day. This custom is now seldom followed.

The *Qing Ming* (清明) Festival

The *Qing Ming* Festival falls about 15 days after mid spring and is usually observed on 5 April. It is reminiscent of All Souls' Day. On this day, it is customary for families to visit their ancestors' graves with offerings. The custom began in the Song dynasty and is still widely observed for sentimental reasons.

Qing Ming actually involves three different customs. Besides visiting ancestors' graves, it is also the time to visit the countryside and hold a picnic. At this time, flowers and plants are usually in their full splendour.

The third custom is that no cooking with fire is allowed on this day. Food must be consumed cold. This is in remembrance of a loyal follower of a prince in exile in the Spring-Autumn period. The follower was accidentally burnt to death. The prince later became king and banned the use of fire on this day in memory of the loyal subject. The "cold food" custom is no longer observed.

The *Duan Wu* (端午) Festival

The *Duan Wu* Festival falls on the fifth day of the fifth lunar month. The festival is the Memorial Day for Qu Yuan (屈原), a well-liked high official, a patriot and an excellent poet in the Chu (楚) state during the Warring States period. He was totally frustrated when he could not get the king to heed his good advice. Upon the instigation of unscrupulous officials, the king exiled him, and he ended up drowning himself in the Mi-Luo River. When the people heard about his suicide, they raced to the river to try to recover his body. That is how the custom of holding a dragon boat race on this day began. The people also threw rice dumplings into the river to feed the fishes so that they would keep away from Qu Yuan's body. That was the origin of the custom of making rice dumplings wrapped in bamboo leaves. The *Duan Wu* customs are still regularly observed even after the passage of some 2,500 years. Qu Yuan's poems showing concern for the country and the people are still found in school textbooks today.

The *Zhong Yuan* (中元) Festival

The *Zhong Yuan* Festival is on the fifteenth day of the seventh month of the Chinese calendar. Another name for the festival is *Yu Lan* (盂兰), a translation from a Sanskrit term, meaning "extreme suffering" or "being hung upside down". It was originally a Buddhist festival.

The story about the origins of the festival goes that Mulian (目连), a disciple of the Buddha, had a very wicked mother who after death was being punished and starved in hell. Mulian was a pious son and wanted badly to save his mother's soul. He was told by the Buddha that his mother's soul could be saved if he provided a sumptuous dinner for a large group of monks at the end of their summer retreat on the fifteenth day of the seventh month. Mulian followed the advice and gained enough merits to transfer his mother's soul to the western heaven. The practice of giving alms to monks was later lost. Now, the festival is mainly about making offerings to hungry ghosts in hell.

The *Zhong Qiu* (中秋) Festival

The *Zhong Qiu* Festival, or the Mid Autumn Festival, probably originated during the Tang dynasty. Also known as the Moon Festival, it is observed on the fifteenth day of the eighth month in the Chinese calendar. On this day, the moon is the brightest and the fullest it will be the entire year.

The celebrations for this festival are held mostly at night. Each family would have a reunion dinner. Mooncakes, confections that symbolise family togetherness, are exchanged between friends and relatives. Children would gather and, each carrying a lantern, roam about the neighbourhood. In the old days, scholars would drink wine, gaze at the moon and compose poetry.

There are several mythological tales about the Moon Festival. One is about the goddess of the moon. A warrior in ancient times had a very beautiful wife named Chang E (嫦娥). The warrior was given a magical drug by the Mother Goddess of Heaven, which when consumed would enable a person to fly to heaven and become a god. The warrior was however reluctant to leave his wife and handed her the drug for safekeeping. On the night of the fifteenth of the eighth month, when the warrior was occupied elsewhere, a student of his tried to force Chang E to hand over the drug. Chang E refused to yield and swallowed the drug herself. She then rose to the sky and flew to the moon where she became the Moon Goddess. It is said one can still see her image in the full moon.

The *Dong Zhi* (冬至) Festival

The *Dong Zhi* Festival, or Winter Festival, is the only traditional festival with an origin that is not associated with a myth or a historical event although it was believed by some that it was the day when the Kitchen God went to heaven to report to the Jade Emperor the conduct of a family.

It falls on 22 or 23 December when the sun is over the Tropic of Capricorn. In the northern hemisphere, it is the day of the year with the least amount of daylight hours, and consequently the longest night. Presumably, it marks the end of harvesting and the beginning of a rest period for farmers.

On this day, it is customary to make sweetened, multi-coloured rice balls, which signify family reunions. How this custom has come about is not clear, but children certainly enjoy eating this food prepared in conjunction with the festival.

THE RESURGENCE OF CHINA

The emergence of China in the twenty-first century as a world power follows more than two centuries of decline. The Chinese, having gone through great adversity, are finally able to find a sense of solace and even renewed pride.

The misery in China during the nineteenth century and the first half of the twentieth century may be attributed largely to foreign predators although the country's own ineptitude and weakness beckoned preying. In the second half of the twentieth century, China's suffering came about as a result of its own bungling and irrationality; no one else is to blame.

Unfortunately, although Mao Zedong's policies were well-intentioned and ultimately aimed at benefiting the people, he was himself not infallible. Dictatorship carried with it a lack of checks and balances, and free discussion. Rule by man rather than rule by law, long practiced in China, led to despotism. All these political deficiencies allowed Mao to act according to his will and inflict serious damage on the nation.

INTERNAL TURMOIL

On 1 October 1949, Mao Zedong proclaimed the founding of the People's Republic of China at Tiananmen. The second half of the century saw China go through intense turmoil, chaos and upheaval. At the end of the civil war between the Nationalists and the Communists, the people expected a change in fortunes and a reprieve from their suffering. Instead, they had to endure a period of hardship with few parallels in Chinese history.

The Great Leap Forward, which began in 1958, was a fanatical drive for industrialisation. Mao ignored realism in favour of willpower based on ideology, and the consequences were disastrous. The creation of the people's communes during this period is an example of a mindless, frenzied attempt to fulfil communist ideology. Mao was apparently oblivious to the failure of Soviet communes in the early revolutionary period. These mistakes sowed the seeds of the subsequent rebellion against Mao's doctrine.

In 1956, Mao feared that an uprising similar to the revolt against the Communists in Hungary might occur in China. Cunningly, he declared the policy of liberal expression: "Let a hundred flowers bloom and let a hundred ideas contend". Many people took the statement at face value and freely expressed their thoughts, not realising that it was a move meant to "lure the snake out of its cave", as one Chinese idiom would put it. As a result, many who spoke their minds were sent to corrective camps to reset their thinking. Others, military and civilian leaders alike, were dispatched to rural areas to perform physical labour as an example to the people.

In 1966, sensing the rising discontent against him within the Communist party, Mao launched the infamous Great Proletarian Cultural Revolution. Hundreds of thousands of young people, effectively indoctrinated and brainwashed, were made "Red Guards" (红卫兵) and turned loose to harass and torment anyone whom Mao disliked. Mao's wife, Jiang Qing (江青) was the power behind Mao in the Cultural Revolution, and she quickly built up her power base. Victims of the Red Guards included Liu Shaoqi (刘少奇), President of the People's Republic of China; Zhu De (朱德), once Commander of the Red Army; Deng Xiaoping (邓小平), General Secretary of the Communist Party of China; Bo Yibo (薄一波), Vice Premier of the State Council; and many other prominent leaders. Numerous intellectuals also suffered the same fate. Unable to withstand the pertinacious torment, many resorted to suicide for relief.

The Red Guards indiscriminately destroyed historical relics and heritage. Premier Zhou Enlai (周恩来) tried to exert a moderating influence during this period of turmoil as the Red Guards turned against anything old: old culture, old thoughts and even old ways of life. The family institution fell apart as children were made to turn against their parents and spouses against each other. Mao's madness practically destroyed a generation of talent and all of the traditional Chinese cultural values.

Mao's wife, Jiang Qing, and her three associates, known collectively as the Gang of Four, exerted influence over the ailing Mao in the last years of his life. They issued orders in Mao's name. Premier Zhou Enlai died of illness in January 1976. He had groomed Deng Xiaoping to take his place, but Mao dismissed Deng from all government and party posts in April. In his waning months, Mao named little-known Hua Guofeng (华国锋) as his successor, to the displeasure of the ambitious Jiang Qing, who had aspired to be his heir. Mao died in September 1976. A month after Hua assumed office, Jiang Qing and the three other members of the Gang of Four were arrested. In 1981, Hua resigned as premier and was succeeded by Zhao Ziyang (赵紫阳), a Deng supporter. Hu Yaobang (胡耀邦), also a Deng man, was Chairman of the Central Committee of the Communist Party of China. Deng himself took over as Chairman of the Central Military Commission. With that shuffling, the Maoist Age came to an end.

A pragmatist, Deng Xiaoping implemented the Open Door Policy to modernise China. Reforms were carried out on all fronts. In contrast to Mao's idea of placing politics in the supreme position or "politics in command", the new policy emphasised economic development or "economics in command". Under Deng, China was well on its way to modernisation. However, the violent suppression of the June 1989 student protest at Tiananmen Square drew strong criticisms over what many nations deemed a violation of human rights and eroded China's newly acquired international standing.

FOREIGN RELATIONS

In 1949, when the People's Republic of China was established, China had, upon surface examination, what seemed to be close ties with Soviet Russia. During the Korean War, in a move that had perhaps been calculated to win Russia's trust or perhaps because China was genuinely concerned that the fall of North Korea would be detrimental to the security of China, one million Chinese 'volunteers' were dispatched across the border to fight the Americans. The cost to China was high. Besides the casualties, China paid 1.35 billion dollars for Soviet equipment and supplies used in the war. Mao himself lost a son.

Nevertheless, Russian premier Stalin and Mao seldom saw eye to eye due to ideological disputes. Stalin considered Mao's method of revolution unorthodox and belittled his achievements. It was said that Stalin called Chinese communists 'radish communists' – red outside and white inside. Mao in turn was bitter at being forced to accept Stalin's rapacious demands for special interests in China such as the joint administration of railways in Manchuria, the joint use of Port Arthur and Darien and other similar privileges. Russia had earlier plotted and supported the independence of Outer Mongolia and made a failed attempt to effect the secession of Xinjiang.

The relationship between the two countries further deteriorated in Nikita Khrushchev's time. Mao was unhappy with Khrushchev's handling of the Cuban missile crisis in 1962, his acceptance of the nuclear test ban treaty and his refusal to support China in its border war with India. At one time, Khrushchev considered destroying China's nuclear installations, and Mao threatened to invade Outer Mongolia.

The Sino-Soviet split widened during the Leonid Brezhnev-Aleksey Kosygin era in Russia. There was bitter dispute over the Sino-Soviet border. China demanded the return of territories taken by Russia. As a result, repeated border clashes broke out in 1967. The tension between the two communist powers did not subside until the later part of the 1980s when the two countries came under the rule of Mikhail Gorbachev and Deng Xiaoping, respectively.

In 1971, American president Richard Nixon astutely spotted an opportunity to lure China away from the Soviet camp. Following Henry Kissenger's secret exploratory visit to China, Nixon went to Beijing in 1972. These American initiatives eventually led to the détente between the two countries and to the return of China to the international community. Taiwan became increasingly isolated as more and more countries recognised the People's Republic of China.

THE TWENTY-FIRST CENTURY

China has transformed itself economically at breakneck speed in the last two decades to come within sight of the First World. The world now expects it to be an economic, political and military superpower in the near future. China seems to deviate more and more from communism every day. Communism increasingly appears to be a mere tool to control the nation and propagate one-party rule. From a pragmatic point of view, most observers would probably agree that this measured political evolution is wise. Democracy is a luxury few economically underdeveloped countries with inadequate mass education can afford to enjoy. China probably has its priorities right in placing economy before Western-style democracy. Democracy in its most commonly recognised form is not perfect; it has been adopted for want of a better system. Thus, the question now is: Will China eventually undergo a smooth transition to democracy or is it likely to regress to mindless despotism? China has been blessed with some capable leaders in the recent years leading up to the present. Its modern, well-educated leaders have been pragmatic and rational. The future will rest on enlightened leadership.

China's place in the international community is in a state of flux. The thorny issue at the moment is Taiwan, specifically regarding its political status as either a sovereign nation or an administrative region of greater China. The United States of America and Japan are both ambivalent and contradictory about their One-China Policy. They want to be on the good side of China for trade and other benefits but refuse to give up the strategic advantage of separating Taiwan from China. They are fearful that Chinese regional dominance will undermine their influence in Asia. It is interesting to note that a friendly relationship between China and Russia may once again be established, presumably to counterbalance the American-Japanese alliance on the issue of Taiwan. The situation is reminiscent of the Three Kingdoms period in ancient China. There are no permanent friends and no permanent enemies among nations.

BIBLIOGRAPHY

樊树志	国史概要	复旦大学出版社, 2000.
安作璋	中国史简编	山东教育出版社, 1998.
黄修荣	中国二十世纪全史	中国青年出版, 2001.
张岂之等	晚清民国史	五南图书出版公司, 1999.
郭孝义	中国近代史	华东师范大学出版社, 1997.
成晓军	中国近现代史365	河北教育出版社, 1998.
贾宗荣	中国现代史	华东师范大学出版社, 1997.
郑浪平	中国抗日战争史	麦田出版社, 2001.
方立	四书五经	世一书局股份有限公司, 2002.
王照	四书五经	星辉图书有限公司, 2001.
宋淑萍	论语	时报出版社, 1998.
杨洪, 等	中庸	甘肃民族出版社, 1997.
陈良运	周易与中国文学	九五国宝重点图书, 1997.

黄卓明	诸子学	北京大学出版社, 2000.
郑 Lin	老子道德经	世界书局, 2002.
赵洪恩	中国传统文化通论	人民出版社, 2002.
李杰	白话史记	哈尔滨出版社, 2003.
祁志祥	佛学与中国文化	学林出版社, 2000.
南怀瑾	中国佛教发展史略 中国道教发展史略	复旦大学出版社, 1987.
飞云居士	细说中国佛教	益群书店出版, 1992.
中华书局编	中国伊斯兰文化	中华书局, 1996.
屈宝坤	中国古代著名科学典籍	商务印书馆, 1998.
赵海明等	中国古代发明	三联书店, 2001.
龚宏	文化大教室	南方出版社, 2002.
桑麻	吉瑞中国节	内蒙古人民出版社, 2004.
李世炜	成语故事	正展出版公司, 2000.
仲跻荣等	郑和	南京出版社, 1990.
梁鉴江	白居易	远流出版公司, 1989.
张国荣	元曲三白首译解	中国文联出版社, 2000.
孙大雨	古诗文英译	上海外语教育出版社, 1995.
高政一	新选古文观止	西北出版社, 1991.
高上泰等	中国历代经典宝库 (青少年版): 论语, 礼记, 孟子, 老子, 诗经, 战国策, 史记, 资治通鉴.	时代文化出版事业公司, 1981.

China Translation and Publishing Corporation and UNESCO. *82 Contemporary Chinese Painters*. 1st edition, Beijing: United Nations Educational, Scientific, and Cultural Organisation, 1986.

Craig, Albert M. *The Heritage of Chinese Civilization*. New Jersey: Prentice Hall, 2001.

Fitzgerald, C.P. *China: A Short Cultural History*. New York: Frederick A. Praeger Publishers, 1961.

Henricks, Robert G. *Lao-Tzu Te-Tao Ching*. London: Rider, 1991.

Hsü, Immanuel C.Y. *The Rise of Modern China*. New York: Oxford University Press, 2000.

Hua Junwu. *Contemporary Chinese Paintings*. Beijing: New World Publishers, 1984.

Huang, Ray. *China: A Macro History*. New York: M.E. Sharpe, Inc. 1997.

Lawrence, Alan. *China Since 1919: Revolution and Reform*. London: Routledge, 2004.

Levathes, Louise. *When China Ruled the Seas*. New York: Oxford University Press, 1994.

Menzies, Gavin. *1421: The Year China Discovered America*. New York: Harper-Collins Publishers, Inc., 2002.

Morton, W. Scott. *China: Its History and Culture*. New York: McGraw-Hill, Inc., 1995.

Ogburn, Charlton, Jr. *The Marauders*. Woodstock: The Overlook Press, 1959.

Shaughnessy, Edward L. *China: The Land of the Heavenly Dragon*. London: Duncan-Baird Publishers, 2000.

Tuchman, Barbara. *Stilwell and the American Experience in China 1911–1945*. London: Phoenix Press, 1970.

ABOUT THE

AUTHOR

ONG SIEW CHEY received his education in Chinese at Chung Ling High School, Penang, Malaysia. He became interested in Chinese literature in his early school years. He attended the University of California at Berkeley and subsequently the University of Chicago School of Medicine where he obtained his M.D. He was trained in surgery at the University of Iowa Hospitals. Prior to his private practice, he was Professor and Head of Surgery at the University of Singapore.

ACKNOWLEDGEMENTS

The author would like to thank Dr. Teoh Eng Soon, Dr. Kowa Nam Sing and Dr. Charles C.S. Toh for their help and suggestions in writing this book.

INDEX

INDEX